Becoming a "Wiz"
at BRAIN-BASED
Teaching

*As always to Scott, Josh, Marnie, Amy, and Thabu for their love and support;
to the newest member of the family, Jackson Joseph Sprenger, and
to the wizard who started me on my journey, Eric Jensen.*

Becoming a "Wiz"
at BRAIN-BASED Teaching

How to Make Every Year Your Best Year

Marilee Sprenger

Skyhorse Publishing

Contents

Acknowledgments

I t has been a pleasure to create this teaching guide. I am indebted to Faye Zucker for her support as my editor and friend. None of this work would have been possible without the dedicated brain scientists, neuropsychologists, science writers, and brain research translators. Eric Jensen introduced me to this exciting field. There are many brain research interpreters, writers, and presenters whose expertise I would like to acknowledge. They include Bob Sylwester, David Sousa, Bob Marzano, Debra Pickering, Debbie Estes, Martha Kaufeldt, Rick Wormeli, Daniel Schacter, Kathie Nunley, Robin Fogarty, and Gayle Gregory. I now follow my own yellow brick road. I thank all of you devoted and thought-provoking people.

I would like to thank the reviewers of this book. You made me think about ideas, discoveries, and concepts that added to the content of this work. The professional advice was appreciated.

I owe a great deal to "my kids," all of the students I have had the privilege to teach through the years. You and your parents encouraged my work even in the early days when I was considered a rebel in education. I appreciate your support and the feedback I am still receiving.

My friends and colleagues at Two Rivers Professional Development Center put up with my deadlines and my crazy schedule of speeches and workshops. I have learned a lot from you, and I am grateful to work with such special professionals who make a difference by training and supporting educators.

I want to thank the many teachers I have worked with for their support and input. Together we have shared strategies and experiences to make the school journey a better one for children.

I also want to thank my friends who listen to me talk about the brain and help me keep track of myself! You have supported me through the years and have shown me the meaning of friendship. Our journey together has had interesting twists and turns, yet we continue on this path together.

A special thanks to my family: my parents for letting me believe I could do whatever I set out to do; my children for sharing their personal experiences and giving me their unconditional support and love; and Scott, a dedicated husband, wonderful father, best friend, and book editor. You read every word and encourage me to continue to write and speak. You give me the courage to change and the emotional support to try new things, and your focused brain keeps mine focused. You are the Cowardly Lion, the Tin Man, and the Scarecrow all rolled into one!

Skyhorse Publishing gratefully thanks the following reviewers for their contributions to this book:

Arthur Huinker
Professor, Loras College
Dubuque, IA

Kathy Tritz-Rhodes
Principal, Marcus Meriden Cleghorn Elementary
Marcus, IA

Valerie A. Ubbes
Associate Professor, Miami University
Oxford, OH

About the Author

 **Marilee Sprenger** is a professional development consultant who has taught at all levels from prekindergarten through graduate school. She is an adjunct professor at Aurora University, where she teaches brain-compatible strategies and memory courses. For the past 15 years, she has been engaged in raising student achievement using brain-based teaching strategies, differentiation, and memory research. Marilee is a member of the American Academy of Neurology, the Cognitive Neuroscience Society, and the Learning and Brain Society, as well as many education organizations such as the Association for Supervision and Curriculum Development (ASCD) and Phi Delta Kappa. She is the author of *Learning and Memory: The Brain in Action, Becoming a Wiz at Brain-Based Teaching, Differentiation through Learning Styles and Memory, How to Teach So Students Remember,* and *Memory 101 for Educators.* She has written numerous articles and provides staff development internationally. Translating and applying current neuroscience research, cognitive science research, and scientifically based educational research, she assists schools and regions internationally.

You can reach her at:

5820 Briarwood Lane
Peoria, IL 61614
Phone: (309) 692-5820
E-mail: brainlady@gmail.com
Web Site: http://www.brainlady.com

Introduction

"The road to the City of Emeralds is paved with yellow brick," said the Good Witch, "so you cannot miss it."

I am speaking at a national conference. It is an educational gathering with various topics and presenters. It is lunchtime and I am in a long line of participants purchasing a quick sandwich before my next presentation.

The woman behind me taps me on the shoulder, "Do they have turkey up there? I'm not going to eat ham again. Yesterday, all they had left was ham."

I look ahead and see a tray of turkey sandwiches. "I think you're safe in this line today. There appears to be at least one full tray of turkey."

"Hey, aren't you that brain person?" she asks. "You talk about the brain and the classroom, don't you? I thought I saw your name in the program book. My school studied the brain stuff last year. This year we're bringing in people to talk about reading and other stuff like differentiation."

"What do you think of the brain research applications?" I ask. "Did you find any success following the brain-based teaching principles?"

"Now, which ones were those? I tried to use some of the strategies on Fridays. That seems to be my best day to try something new," she decides. "Guess this year, I'll switch to something else. Maybe that differentiation stuff."

My heart skips a beat when I hear this. I am about to try to explain how these philosophies connect when the teacher with this woman begins to speak. "Now, Doris," she says, "You never really gave the brain research a chance. It is based on the same philosophies that differentiation is. In fact, I think differentiation is a spin-off of brain research."

"I have to agree with you. Creating a brain-compatible classroom includes differentiating content, process, and product. When I began, it seemed an overwhelming task. But that was years ago, before many people had become translators and interpreters of the brain research. Why, it wasn't very long ago that we didn't even realize the brain had anything to do with learning!" I joke.

The two teachers laugh. We continue through the line and sit together to continue our conversation. Their principal and two other teachers join us.

"I'm sure you understand that with No Child Left Behind, we had to change our focus," Mr. Phillips, the principal begins. "We had one of you brain people out last year, but the teachers didn't really get into it as much as I thought they would."

"How many professional development opportunities on brain-compatible teaching were offered?" I ask.

"Well, it was just the opening day staff development program. After that we had to use all of our staff development days on other things. We're a small district and don't have much money."

"It's a journey," I say quietly. Then more loudly, "It's a journey. One exposure is not going to make a difference. If you want to see change, staff development has to be ongoing. Baby steps at first. Trying something out and seeing if it works. Understanding why it works so you do it again. It's an amazing voyage.

"I was struggling with my students and my sanity. Large classes with students from diverse backgrounds. Brain research saved my life. Or at least my career. I had to dig for information and basically train myself. Now there are all kinds of literature, conferences, and experts in the field who can help your teachers. Brain-compatible teaching is part of the big picture. It's not the only thing, but it is certainly one of the roads to raising student achievement.

"Please don't give your faculty a 'spray and pray' professional development experience. Choose a path and take them on a journey that will affect all of you, personally and professionally. Offer your students the opportunity to learn the way their brains learn best!" I realize that I have attracted some attention from nearby tables. This is not usually my style, and I compose myself. I still look directly at the administrator and smile.

"Well, you are passionate about this, aren't you? If my teachers were that passionate about teaching, I would be pleased," Mr. Phillips says.

"Perhaps you can lead them to a philosophy that will make them passionate about what they do. Support them and guide them with the practical classroom activities and strategies that will give you all a fresh outlook.

"My approach is simple. I compare it to the characters in *The Wizard of Oz*. It makes sense to me. The Cowardly Lion represents the stress that students have to deal with—the stress that teachers have to help control if learning is going to take place. The Tin Man represents the emotional systems in the brain. If we don't deal with our students' emotions, long-term memory can be a problem. And the Scarecrow wants a brain. He's actually thinking about his thinking. That's the metacognition we are after. Higher levels of thinking are possible if we deal with the whole child. Understanding and applying how the brain functions, how memory works, and what the brain needs is what makes a classroom brain-based. Believing that every child is unique and learns differently—and then taking the suggestions of those who have applied these concepts in the classroom and trying them yourself—that's what makes a difference."

"Well, what's Dorothy represent?"

"And the witch? Are the Munchkins representing those students who have different styles of learning?"

"Is the wizard representing the brain?"

There is a barrage of questions from the group I am talking to and a few others from surrounding tables. I sit back and prepare for a long discussion.

The formulation of this analogy took years of researching what the neuroscientists, neuropsychologists, and geneticists were discovering.

The brain-imaging techniques have offered us a multitude of information that was impossible to ascertain when I began my own journey. We can see the living brain as it works and makes connections through **PET (positron emission tomography)** scans, **functional magnetic resonance imaging (fMRI), SPECT scans,** and other technologies (see Table I.1). Functional magnetic resonance imaging has begun to be the most used imaging due to its low invasiveness, lack of radiation exposure, and relatively wide availability.

But it takes more than brain imaging to understand the brains of the many students who pass through our doors. I have learned much in my years of studying brain research, not only about the parts of the brain but also something more important. I have learned that some of the strategies I was using that worked weren't necessarily good for kids. I was trying to tame those lions and tigers and bears with threats and wielded my power of homework or grades to prove who was in control. I was trying to force learning, when all I had to do was create an atmosphere that would allow it to happen. And there were times when I was teaching and no one was listening, because emotionally it just wasn't possible for them to do so.

Although I am now much more confident as a teacher and an interpreter of brain research, there are days when I must face the fact that even though this information is second nature to me, and even though I see it as vital for the schools, the Wicked Witch is still fighting those lions and tigers. The knowledge of some of my successes—students returning to my room just to sit and feel safe, letters and calls about how much they remember from my classes and how it has helped them in high school and college, and standardized tests scores that go up—keep me on this path toward making others aware of the possibilities we have when we understand the brain.

Table I.1   Common Types of Brain Imaging

CAT: Computed Axial Tomography	This type of scanning uses a series of X-rays of the head taken from many different directions. It is typically used for quickly viewing brain injuries, but the scan can also show areas of change.
fMRI: Functional Magnetic Resonance Imaging	This scan relies on the paramagnetic properties of oxygenated and deoxygenated hemoglobin to see images of changing blood flow in the brain associated with neural activity. This allows images to be generated that reflect which structures are activated (and how) during performance of different tasks.
PET: Positron Emission Tomography	After radioactive glucose is injected into the bloodstream, areas of the brain that are burning the most energy show up in reds and yellows in a scanning device. Blues and greens show less activity. In this way scientists can see what areas of the brain are required for certain functions as they ask participants to perform.
SPECT: Single Photon Emission Computed Tomography	SPECT is similar to PET. It uses gamma-ray emitting radioisotopes and a gamma camera that actually shows areas of metabolism. On a SPECT scan, one sees areas that look like holes in the brain, but they are actually areas not metabolizing properly.

I am still making my own journey. There have been many bumps in the road, and I have to remind myself about how to tame my own personal lions. While writing the first edition of this book, I faced my biggest challenge. I was diagnosed with breast cancer. It was devastating, and I had to cope with another journey. As it did to the Cowardly Lion, the stress response overwhelmed me. I was a member of a club that I hadn't wanted to join. Did I have the skills I needed to handle this situation? Amazingly, many of the concepts presented here were helpful to me. Controlling my stress led me to the Tin Man. I needed to use my emotional intelligence when dealing with my loved ones. I needed my children to understand and be calm. I needed the support of my family and friends. I needed a passion for life for myself. Just as the Scarecrow wanted a brain, my understanding of the brain and stress allowed me to make decisions about my attitude, my medications, and my health. I discovered that what I was doing in my classroom could have lifelong and life-altering effects. I hadn't wanted to give these strategies this particular test, but I was relieved to discover that they passed. Like Dorothy, I had to follow a path I had not personally chosen. I had to conquer the Wicked Witch in me as I learned to control my state of mind. And as others gathered close to offer support, I knew there was no place like home.

I continue to use my knowledge about the brain as I face stressful situations. Having this information has affected my classroom, my personal life, and, I hope, the lives of many students who were in my care. I can happily say with this second edition that I am now a seven-year survivor. I look forward to continuing research to help us all lead longer, better lives and to assist others who have their own struggles. This book is for anyone who feels that his or her personal journey is ongoing and wants to use current research to broaden and enhance the trip down the Yellow Brick Road. Undergraduates, new teachers, and veterans will find information and strategies to boost their self-confidence and that of their students. Brain-based teaching is a philosophy that forms a framework for all learners.

There are several reasons for this second edition. The ongoing research has made compelling discoveries that support my continued goal of changing schools from institutions that encourage students to have classroom-compatible brains to institutions that encourage teachers to have brain-compatible classrooms. Specifically, you will find that I have made the following changes:

- Added information on the brain and poverty
- Began with the end in mind by discussing brain-compatible assessment in Chapter 2
- Increased information about how to utilize multiple intelligences
- Created a separate chapter devoted to memory and how to get information into long-term memory to make it accessible
- Introduced the revised Bloom's Taxonomy and how to take students from lower levels of thinking to higher levels
- Updated information on sleep and nutrition
- Added more stories and examples
- Expanded the glossary, and set each word listed in the glossary in boldface the first time it appears in the text
- Used Toto to point out pullout quotes

1 The Journey

The Brain Goes to School

It is a long journey, through a country that is sometimes pleasant and sometimes dark and terrible.

—The Good Witch of the North

It is my first day at a new school. I am both nervous and excited. Even though I consider myself a veteran teacher, I am somewhat apprehensive as I look around my new room. I have several minutes before my students arrive, so I dash into the teachers' lounge to meet my colleagues.

When I enter the small, cluttered room, three teachers are seated and chatting. They look up and smile. "You must be Marilee. You're taking Paula's class," one of them says.

"That's right," I reply. "I'm really looking forward to this."

"Don't take them on any field trips!" all three teachers say simultaneously. "They haven't been out of the building since kindergarten."

I am mildly shocked as I rethink this new position. These children are now in sixth grade. If I keep this job, I will have them for seventh and eighth grade, too. What have I gotten myself into? I quickly decide to disregard what the teachers have told me. After all, I've been around long enough to know how to handle students. The class can't be that bad!

The bell rings, and the students enter the building and go to their respective rooms. I stand at the door to greet them. I am suddenly overwhelmed by the fact that there are so many of them—and so many boys! When they all get settled, I start to take attendance. I call out their names to try to connect names and faces. As I finish, I realize that I have 32 students, and 20 of them are boys. Four rows of eight desks look endless in the narrow room.

Oh, well, no problem. It is time to get started. I quickly introduce myself and give them a little background. As I am sharing, one of the Davids (there are two) gets up out of his seat and goes to the pencil sharpener. I immediately stop in midsentence. "Excuse me; I am talking, so you will have to sharpen your pencil later." He smiles and returns to his seat. I continue.

Seconds later, David #2 goes to the trash can with some paper that he crumples on his way. The noise and the movement are very distracting. "I'm sorry, but no one should be out of his seat," I state in no uncertain terms. No sooner do I have that out than two boys start scuffling in the back of the room. "Hey, hold on there!" I shout, to no avail. David #1 runs back to the scuffling boys and joins in. A cheerleading squad of both boys and girls suddenly develops, chanting, "Scott, Scott, Scott . . ."

As I hurry to break things up, my mind is racing and my anger rising. The principal hears the chanting from her office next door and comes running in.

"What in the world is going on here?" she demands.

I want to be anywhere else besides my classroom. I realize without a shadow of a doubt that I'm not in Kansas anymore!

For weeks, I am near tears as I leave the building each day. I try desperately to get those 32 kids to behave the way I want them to, but nothing works. Finally, I realize that if they aren't going to change, then I must.

My research begins: right-brain/left-brain classes, discipline classes, parenting classes, reading about music to soothe the soul, and reading Howard Gardner's *Frames of Mind* (1985) I finally have enough ammunition to begin to deal with my situation. I work hard and see some improvements.

In the summer of 1992, my life changes. I take a course from Eric Jensen on brain-compatible teaching strategies. During the week, Eric and I talk about my research and what I have learned from him. He asks me if I'd like to learn how to facilitate the class I just finished. I promptly say "No." I was born and raised in Peoria, went to college in Peoria, and married my high school sweetheart. It scares me to death to think about a dramatic career change.

The class ends on Friday, and I go home thinking about my decision not to take Eric up on his offer. I begin to pout. My husband, Scott, says the words that made the difference: "If you don't go, nothing will ever change." That both scares and motivates me. I call Eric and begin my training. I have no intention of teaching the material to other teachers. I just want to learn as much as I possibly can about brain-based learning.

Some extraordinary things happen the following year. I put all the strategies to the test. They all work. Students are happy. I am happy. Parents are happy. Test scores go up. I feel as though I have covered more material in-depth than ever before.

This is too good to keep secret. It is time to share this information. I begin teaching classes for educators during the summers and on weekends. The classes are well attended. As I continue my research, I realize that my challenge is to keep up with the latest discoveries. My classroom becomes a laboratory of sorts. I research carefully to be certain that nothing I try could be in any way harmful. I find myself loving my work as well as my students. They appear to be happy and eager to learn.

Brain research is too important to keep to myself.

The questions I have struggled to answer through the years are "What does every child need from me and from school?" "What can I do to relieve stress in the classroom?" "How can I help students get along with each other?" "How can I help students learn more easily?"

Life is a journey, and school is a major part of the journey for children. To understand how some of our children manage to withstand the journey, how some of them master the journey, and how others succumb to the stress and fail, I first need to gain an understanding of how the experience affects the brain, and how the brain affects the experience.

THE QUESTIONS AND THE RESEARCH

When I begin studying the differences between students' responses to and at school, I am curious as to why some fare better than others. I am also amazed at the children considered at risk who thrive and become successful. What do these kids have, and where did they get it?

Is It Nature or Nurture?

The question of genetics versus environment has been asked and answered in different ways for decades. The Human Genome Project (HGP) was finally completed in 2003. This joint project of the U.S. Department of Energy and the National Institutes of Health truly became a worldwide project with assistance coming from countries all over the globe. The goal of the project was to *identify* all the approximately 20,000–25,000 genes in human DNA, determine their sequences, have the information stored for further research, find and improve tools for analysis, transfer the information to the private sector, and examine the legal and moral issues that presented themselves as a result of the project. The examination of the data will continue for many years, and the results are promising. For instance, in March of 2004, sequencing of Chromosomes 13 and 19 was completed. These two chromosomes relate to such things as breast cancer and repairing DNA from exposure to radiation (HGP, 2003). As the project continues, we can hope that new discoveries will aid us in understanding why our students sometimes have difficulties with learning and memory.

We are born with sets of genes that act as blueprints for some of our development. They are responsible for the colors of our eyes, the shapes of our noses, and the migratory patterns of our brain cells (Hyman, 1999). Are they also responsible for our behavior? Research has been ongoing, with many interesting results. In the search to understand intelligence, studies show that from 50 to 60 percent of intelligence is determined by genetics. That leaves approximately 50 percent to be affected by environment and experience.

As Dean Hamer and Peter Copeland (1998) explained in their book, *Living With Our Genes,* molecular biology discoveries suggest that genes are the most powerful factor in our behavior, yet some traits can be changed, controlled, or modified. We can be shaped by our environments and by individual experiences. Biology doesn't have to be destiny. Genes don't necessarily predict any absolute fates; they can be amplified or stifled by situations (Hayden, 2000).

Biologists have made discoveries that suggest genes are the most powerful factor in our behavior, yet there are traits that can be changed, controlled, or modified. We can be shaped by our environments and by individual experiences.

According to Nobel Prize winner and neuroscientist Eric Kandel, genetic and developmental processes specify the cells that connect to each other, but they do not specify the exact strength of those connections. Environmental possibilities, such as learning, play a significant part in the strength of those connections. In fact, those environmental factors have the power to turn genes off and on. It is this research that should make teachers aware of the power we truly have over changing the brain.

How Do They Cope?

I have always enjoyed the work of Dr. Robert Sapolsky. He continues his research at Stanford University studying stress and its effects on the brain. He has followed the brain and body reactions to chronic stress and made some amazing discoveries. People who exercise show lower levels of stress hormones in their bodies when they encounter potentially stressful situations. Exercise appears to be a factor in coping. When people know they have options, they also feel less stress. This goes along with feeling a sense of control in your life. The knowledge that you can handle a situation or change it alters your reaction.

One morning, a student said to me (about another teacher) "Uh-oh, Mrs. Phillips is wearing a skirt today. She must be in a bad mood." I chuckled at this comment, but the student had learned that this particular teacher dressed to fit her emotional state. The student knew she would have to be very careful not to upset her teacher that day. This measure of predictability enabled the student to cope.

Social interaction is critical to a healthy approach to tough situations. Having someone to talk to or share circumstances with allows for easier management of one's life. In some studies, two groups of mice were given mild electrical shocks. Within the experimental group, a mouse was given a warning that the shock was coming, a piece of wood on which to chew, or a fellow mouse to share the experience. The mice in this group were found to have lower levels of stress hormones in their systems than those in the control group with none of these variables (Sapolsky, 2004).

We can look further into the effects of stress on particular areas of the brain. The **hippocampus,** which is needed for the consolidation of long-term memories, is negatively affected by stress. Chronic stress can cause the hippocampus to lose cells and shrink. This could cause a student to have difficulties storing new memories and therefore have difficulty in school.

A lower incidence of illness has been found in people who have more and varied social interactions throughout the day. Although we might believe that being in contact with more people exposes us to more germs and illnesses, studies reveal the opposite. Simple gestures of support from others can also lower hormonal responses in stressful situations. Stress hormones are known to interfere with infection-fighting immune cells (Sternberg, 2000). Students who have positive social interactions may remain healthier and show better school attendance, which would positively affect their academic performance.

How Does Poverty Affect Resiliency?

As Sapolsky (2005) and others continue their work, they have directed themselves in another important path. What does poverty do to our ability to cope? How does it affect our health? What makes it worse? And what can we do to make it better?

Those in poverty may experience more stress and stress-related problems if they feel as though they have little control over the stressors in their lives, lack predictability about the duration and intensity of the stress, have few outlets for the frustration involved in the stress, and lack social support. Wilkinson (2000) suggested that the surest way to feel poor is to be constantly made aware of that poverty.

The strength of a child's resilience appears to have greater effect on school performance than the child's socioeconomic status.

The strength of a child's resilience appears to have a greater effect on school performance than the child's socioeconomic status. So, too, do the

universal powers of three protective factors: caring relationships, high expectations, and opportunities to participate and contribute. These factors have been
researched and have guided programs for the past decade (Benard, 2004).

What Do Other Experts Say?

Bonnie Benard (2004) has compiled much of the resiliency research in
her book *Resiliency: What We Have Learned*. In this wonderful overview of
two decades of study, she outlines four categories of personal strengths:
social competence, problem solving, autonomy, and a sense of purpose.
These broad categories include many manifestations of resilience that can
certainly be enhanced in varied environmental situations. Not only are
these important in all cultures, they are also important across gender lines
(Werner & Smith, 2001). Table 1.1 illustrates these traits and the subtraits
considered part of them.

Emmy Werner has studied large groups of people over the course of many
years. Her work in Hawaii has added much vital information to the knowledge
of coping skills. Her findings from studying a group of high-risk children as
she followed them through to adulthood shed some light on this topic. Of these

Table 1.1   Personal Strengths for Resiliency, According to Benard (2004)

Social Competence	Problem Solving	Autonomy	Purpose
Eliciting positive responses from others	Planning	Positive identity	Goal direction
	Flexibility: Seeing alternatives	Sense of control	Achievement
Interpersonal connection and relationship building	Resourcefulness	Self-efficacy: Belief that you have power, even if you don't	Motivation
	Critical thinking and insight		Creativity
		Mastery	Imagination
Empathy and caring			Optimism and hope
		Adaptive distancing	
Compassion and forgiveness			Sense of meaning
		Self-awareness	
		Humor	

at-risk children, those who grew to be successful adults had several protective factors going for them. The study found that factors necessary to overcome obstacles include an internal locus of control, interaction with the environment in a physical manner, assigned responsibility, age-appropriate reading skills, and a variety of types of support. The support should come both from within the family and from outside the family. Children who experience these conditions often prove to be resilient. The studies also suggest that even if parents are remote and inaccessible, a child can still thrive with the care and concern of other adults. Children need to develop trust, autonomy, and initiative (Werner & Smith, 1992). If children possess these protective traits, they seem to handle unpredictable situations and scenarios that put them at risk.

Age-appropriate reading skills are critical to the educational process. Educators and scientists are working on this problem. Currently with No Child Left Behind, the work of Sally Shaywitz has come to the forefront. Her book, *Overcoming Dyslexia* (2003), defines dyslexia and other reading problems. She offers suggestions for reading curriculums that she feels are scientifically based and will provide needed content for students with these problems. Dr. Paula Tallal, of Rutgers University, works with children who are language learning impaired. Her work, along with that of Dr. Michael Merzenich, includes developing a computer software program that slows down the phonemes and enables the students to discriminate between sounds. Difficulty in hearing those sounds interferes with a child's reading ability (Tallal, 1999). Pat Lindamood and Nancy Bell have developed a program that makes students aware of how sounds feel when they say them. They also help students visualize what they have read, to help them remember (Kantrowitz & Underwood, 1999). The results of the National Reading Panel (2000) studies have helped many districts focus on the five important

Building vocabulary will build background knowledge.

components of reading: phonemic awareness, phonics, fluency, vocabulary, and comprehension. Through this research and the research on building background knowledge (Marzano, 2004), which suggests that vocabulary and silent sustained reading will help build connections more quickly than any other strategies, the opportunities for raising reading achievement are vast. The work of these researchers and practitioners may help us fill the need for age-appropriate reading skills.

William Glasser has written several books on the subject of what individuals need to thrive in this world. He found that the five essential needs include survival, power, fun, freedom, and a feeling of belonging. With these elements, children can function at their peak. Throughout their lives, they are striving to fulfill these basic needs, and their behavior is dependent on whether or not they do so. If they are unable to meet one or more of the needs, the behavior we see in the classroom is whatever the child thinks will accomplish the task of meeting them. In a school setting, both teacher and child must have these needs met for a satisfying learning experience (Glasser, 1992). Ideally, these fundamental ingredients must be present in all areas of life.

I have always been fond of what Dr. H. Stephen Glenn (1990) had to say about children, self-esteem, and self-reliance. He outlined what he considered to be the greatest human needs. Children, as well as adults, must feel they are a necessary part of something. Personal potency is a need to feel as though one matters in the world. Children want to influence their own destinies and will relate this in some way through their behavior. They want some control. Relationships that enable feelings to be shared and ideas to be respected are compelling factors. Children want to be listened to and understood. If they do not have these needs met by adults, they will go to their peers. This is not always an ideal situation. When problems arise, an experienced person is usually more helpful. Finally, children must feel that their lives have significance and that what they do matters.

A study of hardy adults produced interesting results. The adults lost their jobs and were followed to observe how they managed this traumatic situation. Those who did well actually found the circumstances challenging. They faced matters head-on. These people also showed commitment in their lives. They were dedicated to their families, friends, and employers. They had strong relationships with others and, similar to the previous findings, an internal locus of control. Because of these protective factors, they knew the situation was within their control and that they could solve the problem (Kobasa, 1979; Sylwester, 1995).

The McCormick Tribune Foundation (2004) created a wonderful DVD on what to give every child. This one-hour presentation elaborates on the 10 things every child needs. Although the foundation targeted younger children, I found the list compelling. The researchers at the foundation begin with the concept of interaction. Children need to interact with others and with their environment. Children also need to be touched. This is imperative in building parts of the brain and for strong emotional intelligence. Stable relationships are on this list. Children need to have others in their lives on whom they can count. A safe environment, self-esteem, and quality child

Children need to have others to count on.

care continue the list. I believe the next component, play, is one that every person needs. Play is necessary to practice social skills that will be needed in everyday living. Both pretend play and role-play can allow children to learn empathy and create mental models of what course of action to take in social situations. Communication, music, and reading complete the list. I discuss many of these aspects in more detail in later chapters.

My study could not be complete without a review of the resilience factors that Martin Seligman, of the University of Pennsylvania, feels are necessary. He is an expert in the field of optimism, a trait that has been found to be essential for health and longevity (Mahoney & Restak,1998; Seligman, 1990). His research has continued as he shares the philosophy of positive psychology. His project, called the Penn Resiliency Project, teaches elementary students about explanatory style. The way we explain things to ourselves influences the way we respond. Children and young people who were part of the project were found to have less stress and less physical illness (Peterson & Seligman, 2003).

Optimists are healthier and have stronger immune systems than less optimistic people. If child optimists are healthier, they spend more time in school and, as a result of their attendance, may learn more and have better social interactions with others. Choice is another ingredient that has been found to help children thrive. The list concludes with control and social support (Seligman, 1990). Seligman has also studied learned helplessness. I will cover this condition as it relates to the classroom in a later chapter.

Who Can Survive?

A final thought crossed my mind as I was reading the studies and reports on coping skills. At the United States Holocaust Memorial Museum in Washington, D.C., I found a book that listed seven human needs. The millions who survived the Holocaust would know better than the rest of us what is needed to survive. These needs begin with security. One must feel safe in one's environment. For some of our students, our classrooms are their safest surroundings. Acceptance is the second need. Every individual wants to be unique and to be respected for that uniqueness. Research has shown that acceptance of oneself is the first step toward fulfilling this need. Belonging is necessary, because each of us desires to be a member of a society that appreciates us. Fitting in is more important than learning to many of our students. To have the ability to make choices about one's own life, a person must have self-determination. Knowing that he or she can establish goals and carry them out can make a great deal of difference. Structure is a component that gives some predictability. We all would like to have some knowledge of what to expect and what is to be expected of us. These last two needs go hand in hand. We need a purpose in our lives. We need to feel that we contribute to society in a meaningful way, and we want validation for that contribution (Quenk, 1997).

Where Does Emotional Intelligence Fit In?

Taking the results of these studies and the suggestions of the experts, I turned to Daniel Goleman's (1995, 1998a, 1998b; Goleman, Boyatzis, & Mckee, 2002) work with emotional intelligence. He has found that children do not learn well without the emotional and social skills he describes. To deal with others, one must be aware of one's emotions, recognize and understand the emotions of others, be self-motivated, control impulsivity, and be able to handle relationships. In Howard Gardner's (2000) theory of multiple intelligences, these are the interpersonal and intrapersonal intelligences. These skills may be more important than the cognitive skills we teach.

One must be aware of one's emotions and others' emotions to handle relationships.

The ability to cope and be resilient in life is very much influenced by our ability to get along with others. Our society is set up for interaction. In earlier societies, interaction related to physical survival. Today, it is intertwined with emotional survival. Learning is a social event; for any of us to become lifelong learners, we must engage in the process with others.

CONNECTING THE INFORMATION

Several central ideas are repeated in these experts' findings (see Table 1.2). I have taken these strong points, applied them to the current brain research, and outlined brain-compatible teaching strategies to help meet students' needs in the classroom. Throughout my personal journey, I have applied these ideas in my own classroom and spoken to other teachers who have used these and other comparable methods. Students have told me what a difference being in my classroom has made in their lives. I am not proclaiming any miracle cures for our society. I have seen these strategies make teachers' and students' journeys through school become more positive emotional and cognitive experiences.

As I study the current brain research, I know I need to look at the biology of the brain. What is going on in children's heads? What parts of the brain are involved in the ability to overcome obstacles? What chemicals are being released that would make a difference? What are the odds that students could learn the behavior necessary to be resilient and successful?

The field of neuroscience has grown rapidly—the twenty-first century is considered the Century of the Brain by many—and this has brought about exciting discoveries. The money spent on research has brought us closer to cures for neurological diseases and discoveries to aid brain-injured people.

Table 1.2   Research on Coping and Resiliency

Coping Skills	Resilient Children	Hardy Adults
Sapolsky 1. Physical outlet* 2. Choice* 3. Control* 4. Predictability 5. Social support*	**Werner** 1. Feeling of control* 2. Interacting physically with the environment* 3. Assigned responsibility 4. Age-appropriate reading skills 5. Variety of support*	**Kobasa** 1. Challenge 2. Commitment 3. Feeling of control*
Basic Needs	*Resilient Factors*	*Greatest Human Needs*
Glasser 1. Power 2. Fun* 3. Freedom* 4. Belonging* 5. Love	**Seligman** 1. Optimism 2. Choice* 3. Control* 4. Social support*	**Glenn** 1. Personal potency* 2. Control* 3. Relationships* 4. Life has significance
Ten Things Every Child Needs	*Seven Human Needs*	*Personal Strengths*
McCormick Tribune 1. Interaction* 2. Touch 3. Stable relationships* 4. Safe environment 5. Self-esteem 6. Quality child care 7. Play 8. Communication 9. Music 10. Reading	**Holocaust Survivors** 1. Security* 2. Acceptance 3. Belonging* 4. Self-determination 5. Structure* 6. Purpose* 7. Validation	**Benard** 1. Social competence* 2. Problem solving 3. Autonomy 4. Sense of purpose* *Protective Factors* **Benard** 1. Caring relationships* 2. High expectations 3. Participation and contribution

NOTE: Items marked with an asterisk (*) are repeated.

In recent years we have also had disaster. Students killed students and teachers in a number of horrible incidents. Such senseless tragedies need to be understood and prevented in the future. We must be able to understand how our children feel and think and know what we can do to keep them from feeling alienated. One study determined that more than 135,000 students bring weapons to school (Cohen, 1999).

Connections between a child and school and a child and his or her family have been shown to protect against stress, suicidal thoughts, violence, and the use of cigarettes and illegal substances (Klein, 1997). The family has changed. There are many reasons for the changes that have occurred. World War II caused the first of them. At that time, many women went into the cities to do the work that men had traditionally done. This began a deterioration of the extended family. Families who had been living close to relatives now had no one to talk to or turn to for help in raising their children. Aunts, grandparents, or cousins were not available for the children when Mom and Dad were away. Along with the distance of family members came a loss of responsibility. In rural areas, children had been given chores or tasks to perform to help the family run smoothly. In the cities, many lived in apartment buildings where few of these chores needed to be done. Children began to feel less connected to their families and less useful (Glenn, 1989).

Children need to be assigned responsibility.

The trend continues today. Families seek employment opportunities away from their relatives, many families have both parents working, and there are also many single-parent families. The children are left to fend for themselves. Many students get themselves up in the morning, dress, eat, and get themselves to school. For some of them, the morning begins with negative remarks from parents who may be getting ready for work or sleeping in because of a late shift. They carry that negativity to school with them. They may talk to themselves, putting themselves down and wondering why they were ever born. At school, they may turn an innocent incident into something much bigger. For instance, just walking down a crowded hallway could create some shoulder bumping or pushing. This type of student may overreact in such a situation and take the anger or frustration from his home condition out on another student. Perhaps the student will then say something inappropriate to a teacher. By the end of the day, the child could be suspended, because he or she could not handle certain social situations when confronted with them.

Marketing consultants have discovered the needs of the child in the new millennium. They work at developing ideas that could help children meet some of those needs. Realizing that parents are inaccessible to many youngsters, they may design a doll to look like Mom (Adler, 1998)! Companies see a market for such products, because so many children long for human contact, especially from their parents.

If students are not being taught appropriate social and emotional skills at home, it behooves us as educators to teach them at school. What I propose is not a curriculum. It is a philosophy, a belief that students must receive the emotional and academic support they need to thrive on their journeys through school and through life.

> If students are not being taught appropriate social and emotional skills at home, it behooves us as educators to teach them at school.

A few years ago, I received an award from a former student. In the school I taught in at the time, it was a tradition for a senior student council member to give an award to the teacher who most affected his or her life. Tears started streaming down my face when Vinnie handed me the small plaque. The student council advisor read an essay Vinnie had written, which explained why he had chosen to give this award to me. I looked into Vinnie's eyes and remembered a particular day during his eighth-grade year. I was driving to school and saw several students hanging out near a doughnut truck. I smiled and waved, but the boys turned away. When Vinnie came into class, he was more active than usual. As he tried to make himself sit down and be still, I walked over and asked, "What's up, Vince?" He looked into my eyes, and I saw an excited but scared young boy. He continued to jiggle and wiggle in his seat but said nothing.

Later, when I passed him in the hall, he hung his head. I called Vinnie in after school and asked him if he wanted to talk about anything. As he sat with his size-12 feet hanging out into the aisle, tears came to his eyes, and he told me of the doughnut heist. The boys had taken doughnuts off the truck, eaten too many, and been hyped up the entire day. Vinnie's remorse was genuine, and he began to share the rationalizations he had used earlier to convince himself that what he had done was justified. His parents were divorcing. Mom was going back to school and working. Dad was living with a woman who had several children, and he never came around anymore. Vinnie was on his own in the morning and decided this would be a quick and easy way to get breakfast. He looked up at me. "Mrs. Sprenger, are you going to tell?"

I knew I had several options. This was a Catholic school, and I could easily give this information to the priest, and he would handle it. This was one of the hundreds of decisions teachers have to make every day, and I honestly did not know what to do. If Vinnie were my son, Josh, I would have several punishments to dole out, a husband to help make the decisions, and the power to have Josh work off the amount of money he had taken in doughnuts and pay back the doughnut man. Making him worry about whether the doughnut company would press charges was also an option. But this was not my son. This was one of my "kids." I felt as if he was mine when we were at school together and in other social situations when his family was not around. I had to quickly make a choice that I thought would affect Vinnie in a positive way for the future. I wanted to be someone he could trust at this time in his life when he felt others were abandoning him, yet I did not want to encourage dishonesty and theft. I told Vinnie to come in after school for the following week. He was to bring Joey, one of the other students I had recognized, with him.

I put the boys to work. They cleaned, dusted, vacuumed, moved books and bookcases, and cleaned the toilets in the school. When others asked why I was having them do this, I simply replied, "These boys owe me." When the week was up, I took the boys and the money I thought they had earned to the doughnut shop. The boys apologized and paid the owner. They promised not to do anything like it again. I explained to the man that the boys had worked hard for the money and I was willing to vouch for them. There would be no future heists from these two. We were lucky. The man was kind and thanked us.

I didn't stop there with Vinnie or Joey. The boys often stayed after school, helping with chores or just talking. To my knowledge, they never got into trouble again. I asked the priest to talk to Vinnie about his problems at home, but he seemed to be happier in the classroom than being pulled out for these discussions.

The boys graduated from grade school in May. I wanted to leave one last impression on Vinnie. He had so much potential, and his home life had improved very little. I asked him to lunch during that summer. I picked him up, took him to a nice restaurant, and bought him whatever he wanted. We spoke of his future plans, and I reminded him of his potential and my faith in him.

I didn't see Vinnie for three years after that. I ran into him at a basketball game, where he was watching his girlfriend cheer. He came over and hugged me and said things were going well. He introduced me to his girl: "This is the teacher I had who took me to lunch." They hurried off, and until he walked into my classroom with the plaque, I hadn't laid eyes on him. He was still growing, ready to graduate from high school, and heading for a university.

I took that plaque into my classroom and hung it on the wall, where four others were already hanging. A colleague who had just seen the presentation of the award stuck her head in my doorway. She asked the rhetorical question, "What do you do to those kids?"

Follow me down the Yellow Brick Road and I will show you.

We're Off to See . . .

Brain development and function is the next necessary piece of information to have. This may be a refresher for some of you, but I have added current information that may be of interest.

WIZDOM

Key Points to Ponder

1. The journey through school is filled with uncertainties that educators must address.

2. Educators must keep up with current brain research.

Suggestions

- The overlapping needs appear to be choice, a sense of control, social support, and interaction. Does your classroom provide these?
- What other areas can you support in your classroom? Predictability and safety, assigned responsibility, and emotional and physical outlets may already be incorporated in your learning environment. If they are not, consider how you may include them as you progress through the book.
- As you continue to read, look for specific strategies you would like to try. Incorporate them slowly, one at a time, and let yourself become comfortable with each before you add the next.

2 Building the Yellow Brick Road

Understanding How the Brain Develops and Functions

But it is a long way to the Emerald City, and it will take you many days.

—A Munchkin

My son is married, and we are awaiting the birth of my first grandchild. This is a high-risk pregnancy, and, as a result, we are very aware that on a daily basis miracles are occurring. I provide Josh and Amy with brain books, articles, and videos. Ultrasound pictures are being taken on a weekly basis, and we watch this child grow and change. We also discover that Amy is having a boy!

What we are seeing is the outside. On the inside, the baby's brain is rapidly changing. Amy is surprised to find out that her early pregnancy nausea may have been protecting his brain. By the 26th day of her pregnancy, the neural tube that would become his brain had closed. The top of the tube would develop into his brain, and the rest would become his spinal cord. By the sixth week, differentiation began to take place, and the major brain structures started to take shape. Genetics played a part in this process. Genes provide a program with a sequence of events that guide the neural development. According to research, the quality of a baby's development is also shaped by his or her environment.

I explain to Amy and Josh that the genetic portion of this process is like the Yellow Brick Road. If Dorothy and her friends follow it, they will reach their destination. The environment consists of the interventions they encounter on their journey. These can cause delays and make the path different for them than it might be for someone else. Amy's emotions and movements and the foods she eats are all part of the baby's environment.

> Amy is just heading into her 24th week. The fetus will now have a small chance of survival outside the womb, as the brain stem is capable of directing respiration. But the rest of the brain is still immature. The top layer, the cerebral cortex, is smooth and awaits the chance to grow and fold into the wrinkly structure that we think of when we say "brain" (Eliot, 1999).

BASIC BRAIN STRUCTURE

If his mother's pregnancy goes to full term, 40 weeks, my grandson's brain will weigh about one pound. Even so, it will be very primitive. It will double in weight during the first year of his life and reach about 3 pounds by the time he reaches adulthood. His adult male brain will weigh more than the adult female brain, but size does not seem to affect intelligence. His brain will represent about two percent of his body's weight; however, it uses from 20 to 25 percent of his body's energy. In other words, it will burn about one-fourth of the calories he eats. It will be the consistency of loose gelatin, and, although the outer layer has been called *gray matter*, it is really a pinkish-brown color.

The human brain differs from the brains of other species in two important ways. First, the human brain has a larger cognitive area, and humans have the ability to use it for higher-order thinking. Second, in most other species, the offspring are born with almost fully developed brains, whereas the human brain requires nurturing for 18 to 20 years (Sylwester, 1997a). This is not full development, however. It has recently been discovered (Talaga, 2000) that the brain is not fully developed until sometime between the ages of 22 and 35!

The reptilian brain is set for survival.

Metaphors, analogies, and similes have been shown by researchers to assist with memory. The Wizard of Oz/brain analogy, therefore, is helpful in understanding and remembering how the brain works. The Cowardly Lion is representative of the **reptilian brain** or R complex as described in the very earliest days of connecting the brain to learning by Dr. Paul MacLean (Hannaford, 2005). The **brain stem** was referred to as the reptilian brain, because it directs functions that are simply instinctive and very primitive. This area regulates functions such as breathing, heart rate, metabolism, and the waking and sleeping cycles. If we look at the structures in the reptilian brain, we find the medulla oblongata, the pons, and part of the reticular activating system. The reptilian brain is set for survival. In a crude sense, it is in charge of the rest of the brain's responses. It is through the reticular activating system that chemicals are released to alert the **amygdala** and **hypothalamus,** structures in the limbic area of the brain that actually set off the fight-or-flight response. In an evolutionary manner, it is thought that the reptilian brain developed first. It appears to be very hardwired, ritualistic, and repetitive. It is often called an instinctual brain. The Cowardly Lion jumps at any unusual or new stimuli in his life. It is the reticular activating system in his brain stem that alerts the rest of his brain to these occurrences. His jumping and hiding are characteristics of stress.

Figure 2.1 shows both the reptilian brains and other parts of a fully developed brain. The region above the brain stem is called the **limbic brain.** This area is touted as controlling the emotions. It does much more than that; it also helps in the storage of many of our memories. The limbic system, as it is sometimes referred to, contains the hippocampus, amygdala, **thalamus,** hypothalamus, **pineal gland, pituitary gland, mammillary bodies,** and the **cingulate gyrus.** The thalamus sorts information coming into the brain, and the hypothalamus regulates information from within the body. When factual information enters the brain and is important enough to be stored in long-term memory, the hippocampus is the structure that allows this to happen. If the

Figure 2.1   Parts of the Brain

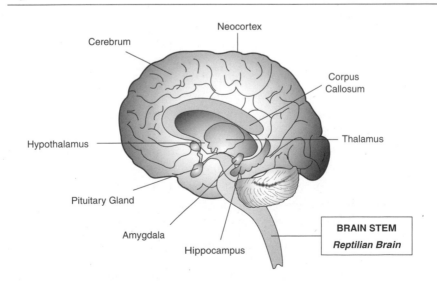

NOTE: This figure shows the brain stem, limbic structures, and neocortex.

information is emotional and is to be stored, the amygdala is in charge of this storage process. The amygdala is always filtering incoming information for emotional content. When it finds this type of content, it will communicate to areas throughout the brain that the information should be attended to and stored. The limbic system is often called the mammalian brain. It is the second brain to evolve and has learning capacities that the reptilian brain does not. Dr. Paul MacLean called it the *emotional brain* (LeDoux, 2002). This system is represented by the Tin Man, who wanted more than anything to have a heart so he could feel.

The reptilian brain and the limbic brain have been connected with the decision-making process that the body goes through when encountering stimuli. It is thought that the primitive area of the brain looks at information to determine whether to run, fight, or mate (Sylwester, 2000). The definitive solution lies with the two systems working together, sometimes making split-second decisions for survival.

The next layer of the brain is the **cerebrum.** This is divided into the right and left hemispheres. The cerebrum itself is often referred to as our white matter because it is white from a coating of **myelin,** the fatty substance that covers some brain cell connections. The cerebrum is actually a collection of the connections that send messages from the brain to the body. The two hemispheres are connected by a band of fibers called the **corpus callosum.** This band enables communication between the two sides of the brain. Some studies suggest that a woman has a larger corpus callosum than a man and therefore is able to switch back and forth between hemispheres more quickly (Gurian & Ballew, 2003).

The corpus callosum is a band of fibers connecting the two hemispheres.

The cerebrum has a thin cover, about one-eighth of an inch thick. This is the **neocortex,** which means *new bark.* It is sometimes called the *cerebral cortex* and is the layer that does the thinking. The Scarecrow was looking for a brain so he could think great thoughts. This area is our so-called gray matter. It invents, creates, writes, calculates, and gives us many of the wonderfully human attributes we possess. We know that the left and right hemispheres have different functions. The left hemisphere is in charge of speech, logic, sequence, time, details, and math. The right hemisphere is related to music, art, strong emotional responses, intuition, images, and summarizing. I teach my students to remember that the left hemisphere deals more with parts, whereas the right deals with wholes. These two work together very well to make life complete. I want to note here that although for many years the left-brain/right-brain theory of learning has been disregarded, new research about the differences in male and female brains has again brought the theory to the forefront. Some research suggests that girls have more activity in their frontal lobes, stronger connections between the hemispheres, and language centers that mature earlier than those of boys. Boys, on the other hand, have stronger right hemispheres and are more spatially oriented (Tyre, 2005). These are, of course, generalities. Not all boys and girls would fit this profile.

> I am giving one of my brain research seminars in the Midwest. One of the participants comes to me the day we have finished discussing brain structure. She begins, "I have a story you may want to share at future classes. My son was born with only one hemisphere of his brain." Although I have read about such situations, I had never known anyone who had lived through it. My heart immediately goes out to this woman.
>
> "His left hemisphere was developed, but he had no right hemisphere. His skull was filled with fluid, and the doctors had to give him a shunt to drain some of it."
>
> I wait for her to continue. She had spoken of her child only in the past tense. I do not want to say anything to upset her.
>
> "He is really doing fine now. The left hemisphere took over the functions of the right. His left arm and leg are smaller than his right. He walks with a limp, but when he runs, you can't even tell there is a problem!"
>
> I breathe a sigh of relief. I am eager to ask her a million questions, but I resist. In the continuing conversation, I discover that her son is a senior at the same university that my daughter, Marnie, attends.

Part of the brain's ability to rewire itself when necessary is demonstrated in this fascinating story. The brain works in mysterious ways, but this ability of the brain hemispheres to take over functions has been well documented. The hemispheres of the brain are also divided into lobes. The occipital lobe, at the back of the brain, process visual information. The temporal lobes on the side, above the ears, process auditory information and some memory. The parietal lobe, on the top of the brain toward the back, processes sensory information and does some problem solving. The frontal lobe, at the front of the brain, deals with decisions, planning, creativity, and problem solving. The prefrontal area, which is right behind your forehead, is an important region that deals with emotions, personality, working memory, attention, and learning.

The cerebral hemispheres are divided into four lobes.

We must not forget the *little brain* at the back and beneath the occipital lobe. This is the **cerebellum.** In the past, it was thought to be responsible only for posture and balance, but current research suggests that it stores certain memories and may have other functions as well (Sprenger, 1999). The cerebellum not only helps us navigate our bodies, as in assisting us in getting from point A to point B, it also helps us navigate thought processes. It is thought that when we move and exercise our cerebellum, we are preparing it not only for movement, but also for thinking (Giedd, 2002).

We can look at brain processing simply as it follows a path:

1. Information enters the brain through the senses.

2. All sensory information except the sense of smell goes to the thalamus.

3. The thalamus sorts the information to send it to the various areas in the cerebral cortex.

4. Visual information goes to the visual cortex in the occipital lobe, auditory information goes to the auditory cortex in the temporal lobe, and so on.

5. If the information is important and factual, the limbic structure called the hippocampus catalogs it for long-term memory.

6. If the information is important and emotional, the limbic structure called the amygdala catalogs it for long-term memory.

7. In the neocortex, the information is examined and worked through for pattern and meaning.

THE BUILDING BLOCKS

How does a brain develop? What causes the growth that is seen from conception to birth? It is the individual cells in the brain that grow and migrate to form the specific brain regions.

Just as the bricks are laid in a certain pattern on our yellow brick road, our brain cells find their spots to become the structures and carry out the functions of our brain regions. The brain contains many different kinds of cells. Some types of **glial cells** feed other brain cells. They are nurturing cells and allow the learning cells to work to their capacity. Recent research suggests that glial cells may assist with the transmission of messages. They are sometimes called **interneurons.** Without the glial fiber (see Figure 2.2), the brain cells would not be able to migrate to the appropriate areas (Kunzig, 1998).

 Glial cells are nurturing cells in the brain.

Other work of the glial cells, of which there are several types, includes transporting nutrients, holding neurons in place, and digesting parts of neurons that

Figure 2.2 Neuron Traveling Along Glial Cell Fiber

NOTE: This figure shows a glial cell with a neuron traveling up its fiber to migrate to the appropriate place in the brain.

are incapable of further activity (Chudler, 1999). One type of glial cell provides the fatty substance called myelin that coats parts of other cells (see next section).

The type of cell basic to learning is the *neuron,* or nerve cell. If my daughter-in-law's pregnancy goes to full term, my grandson's brain will include about 100 billion neurons at birth. Many of those neurons are used, but some of them never make connections and remain unused. Because the brain works according to a "use it or lose it" rule, unused neurons may become useless. That is not to say that we lose them altogether; they simply lose their ability to learn (Diamond & Hopson, 1998).

Learning takes place when two neurons communicate. To understand how they communicate, we must first look at the structure of the neuron. The neuron has a cell body. It may begin its life simply, looking something like a ball. When the neuron begins to get information, it grows appendages called **dendrites.** Dendrites receive information for the neuron; they are always looking for information because the brain wants to learn. The dendrites themselves may grow appendages that also have dendritic capabilities. There may be several levels on a single dendrite. It is sometimes hard to see the strong desire of the brain to learn in our classrooms; however, the brain is always searching for meaning.

After information is received, it is sent to the next neuron via a formation called an **axon.** Neurons may have numerous dendrites, but they have only one axon. When two neurons communicate, information goes from the axon of the sending neuron to the dendrite of the receiving neuron (see Figure 2.3). A tree might be a good representation of a neuron. The trunk would represent the axon, and the branches of the tree would be the dendrites. Information enters the branches, goes through the cell body, down the trunk, and out through the roots. Just as the tree has several roots, an axon may grow small appendages, called axon terminals, to help accommodate numerous transmissions.

Figure 2.3   Neurons Communicating

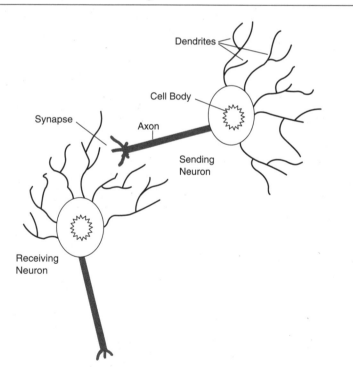

NOTE: When neurons communicate, learning takes place. Information goes out through the axon of the sending neuron, crosses the **synapse,** and attaches to the dendrite of the receiving neuron. The receiving neuron sends the message through its cell body and down its axon to continue the process.

A gap exists between the axon of the sending neuron and the dendrites of the receiving neuron. This space is called a *synapse.* Its purpose is simple. The messages sent from neuron to neuron are chemical. These chemicals, called **neurotransmitters,** must cross the synapse to the next neuron. Many neurotransmitters are found in the brain, and neurons can receive messages from many different neurons; the space allows many messages to be received. When neurons continually communicate with each other, a **neural network** is formed. The more this network is used repeatedly, the more quickly and smoothly the messages are transmitted. When a neuron sends a message to another neuron, it is said to *fire.* If the message I am receiving is "Cows give milk," many neurons must connect for that message to be understood in my brain. As this fact is conveyed throughout my lifetime, these neurons fire together repeatedly. They eventually become so accustomed to firing together that it would be difficult for me to change this information in my brain if I were to discover it to be false. It is often said that neurons that fire together wire together.

> Neurons that fire together wire together.

Coating the Pathways: Myelin

To speed and ensure the transmission of messages, most axons in the brain are coated with myelin, a white fatty substance. The coating actually consists of one type of glial cell, the ogliodendrites, which wrap themselves around the axon. Neurons are leaky, so the myelin seals the axon to prevent the loss of messages. So, neuronal circuits work better once this process is completed (Eliot, 1999). Myelin coats specific brain areas in a developmental fashion. For instance, the coating begins at the back of the brain, and the final bursts of myelination occur in the frontal lobes.

The myelin coating, which has been compared to insulation on electrical wiring, does not cover the axon like a tube (see Figure 2.4). It looks more like link sausages on the axon. This is because messages within the neuron are electrical, and the impulse travels on the outside of the axon in a process called *saltatory conduction* (Chudler, 1998). The message travels down the axon, aided by the white myelin coating, which acts like insulation on an electrical wire. At the tip of the axon, the electrical pulse causes vesicles within the axon to release the message in the form of a chemical neurotransmitter.

To know the brain is to understand the importance of myelin to learning. Until all the areas of the brain are myelinated, there may be difficulties learning in the areas waiting to be developed. The timing and rate of myelination controls the speed at which that brain region learns. Pending the completion

Figure 2.4   Neuron With a Myelin-Coated Axon

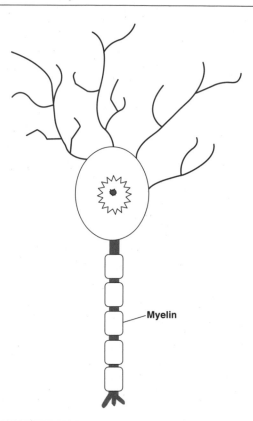

Myelin

NOTE: Neurons are myelinated as part of the development process.

of this process, unmyelinated areas are not working at their optimal level. At birth, the spinal cord and brain stem are almost completely myelinated. After birth, myelination continues in the cerebellum; then the thalamus and parts of the limbic system follow in the first two years of life. The neocortex develops in an irregular manner. In a rapid phase, sensory areas myelinate followed by motor areas. The major lobes—parietal, temporal, and frontal—are still myelinating well into the second and third decades of life. For instance, the prefrontal cortex, the area behind your forehead, is the last area to develop fully. Since the functions of this region include such higher levels of thinking as analysis, synthesis, decision making, and future planning, we realize that some students have difficulty with these skills due to having immature brains. Therefore, it may be necessary, and it is highly recommended, that we continue to introduce information in a concrete manner before advancing to abstractions.

Plasticity

The brain has the amazing ability to change. To indicate this capability, it is said to be *plastic*. **Plasticity** allows the child with only one hemisphere to function almost perfectly and have a normal life. As the brain develops in the womb, the growing neurons travel along the glial fibers to their new homes. These are specific areas of the brain where they will function. For quite some time, however, they remain uncommitted to this space and may be used elsewhere (Neville, 1997). If my grandson is born prematurely and is treated in a dark, womblike environment, he will develop more normal neural connections than preemies treated in standard neonatal intensive care settings. This knowledge comes from another study that suggests that experience can physically change the brain and influence learning (Kotulak, 2004).

> Experience can physically change the brain and influence learning.

The younger the individual, the easier it is for the brain to make changes. However, it is still possible for neurons to take on new responsibilities later in life. This happens when there is brain damage from accidents and stroke. Although neurons may be destroyed by the damage, in some instances, therapy allows the victim to regain some of the lost brain function. Plasticity accounts for learning as well. Researchers Marian Diamond, of the University of California, Berkeley, and William Greenough, of the University of Illinois, have discovered that old rats can grow new dendrites in an enriched environment (Diamond and Hopson, 1998). An enriched environment for a rat includes cage mates and challenging toys. After living in this kind of environment, the rats learned faster and remembered longer. Other researchers, such as Dr. Craig Ramey of the University of Alabama, have carried this research into the human world. Ramey studied children taken from poverty and placed in enriched day care environments that included proper nutrition, stimulation, playmates, and challenging things to do. They showed a remarkable increase in test scores compared with his control group (Blum, 1999).

THE YELLOW BRICK ROAD IS PAVED WITH MESSENGERS

If the neurons are the bricks that become a pathway to learning, the cement that connects them is made up of the dozens of chemical neurotransmitters.

Without them, there is no road, as it is the connections in the brain that create the learning and the memories. Molecules of these transmitters carry messages throughout the brain. Neurotransmitters excite, inhibit, or in some way modulate the activity of neurons. Although many have been identified, there is a handful that are crucial to our understanding of the brain.

Acetylcholine

Involved in many situations, **acetylcholine** is released every time you move a muscle in your body. It activates the muscle fibers. This chemical is also involved with the sleep stage called rapid eye movement (REM). Dreaming occurs during this phase of the sleep cycle. Finally, acetylcholine is very involved with learning and memory. Long-term memories could not be established without its release. In Alzheimer's disease, the production of acetylcholine may be down 90 percent in areas such as the hippocampus. Many of the drugs being developed to fight the symptoms of the disease are designed to produce more acetylcholine in the brain.

Amino Acids

Gamma-aminobutyric acid (GABA) is a neurotransmitter in the brain that reduces anxiety. Because it keeps certain neurons from firing, it is called an *inhibitory* neurotransmitter. GABA is found in abundance in the prefrontal cortex. Its job is to send a "no" signal to neurons that should not fire. **Glutamate** is the most abundant *excitatory* neurotransmitter. It sends the "yes" message to neurons to make them fire. "Yes" and "no" chemistry sends many of the messages in the cortex. Glutamate is formed in the hippocampus and is responsible for all the messages in that structure. This important chemical can perform both positive and negative functions in the brain. When damage is done to the brain, such as from a stroke, a heavy dose of glutamate is released from the neurons and can eventually kill other brain cells (Pert, 1997). It has also been found to work with **cortisol,** a stress chemical, and to cause damage to the hippocampus (McEwen & Lasley, 2001).

Dopamine

This is the reward chemical. **Dopamine** is the neurotransmitter with the attitude, "If a little is good, a whole lot must be better." Released from a brain stem structure, the substantia nigra, dopamine is critical to voluntary movement. A lack of dopamine causes the symptoms of Parkinson's disease, such as tremors and stiff movements.

Dopamine is also vital in helping you direct attention and make decisions. When working memory is trying to make a decision, dopamine inhibits other stimuli in the prefrontal cortex. After considering options in a possible emergency situation, dopamine inhibits the leftover possibilities once the final decision is made. It also balances the excitatory and inhibitory chemical conditions in this area, which affords working memory the opportunity to comprehend. An imbalance of dopamine in the prefrontal cortex could cause disruptions and incompetence (Niehoff, 1999). This is one example in which **norepinephrine** and dopamine work on the same situation. Norepinephrine is the chemical that made you aware of the problem, and dopamine helps you solve it.

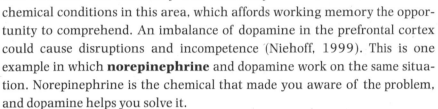

Dopamine is the reward chemical and also helps direct attention.

A lack or imbalance of dopamine in the prefrontal cortex can be a problem for some students. Because this is the area for decision making and attention, these students may have difficulty planning ahead on simple tasks, such as remembering needed supplies for class (Ratey, 2001). As a result, they may cause some disruption. Because of the need for dopamine, they may also seek movement and thrills. Each of these activities would cause the release of the chemical.

Endorphins and Enkephalins

These two sets of chemicals are examples of peptide neurotransmitters. They are found in several areas of the brain and are also produced by the pituitary gland and released in the body as hormones. They are both part of the brain's endogenous morphine system, which consists of chemicals made in the brain and body to alleviate pain. In survival situations, many people report feeling no pain from injuries during the period of time in which they were escaping danger. This is due to the work of these analgesics. This same "numbness" may be felt in emotionally stressful situations (Niehoff, 1999). When **endorphins** and **enkephalins** enhance the release of dopamine, they are also involved in pleasure (U.S. Department of Health and Human Services, 1993).

Norepinephrine

This neurotransmitter is sometimes called noradrenaline. It is manufactured in an area of the brain stem called the locus coeurelous and is released in a smooth, easy rhythm until something alarming occurs. At that point, the chemical is released in abundance and floods the hippocampus, hypothalamus, amygdala, and the cerebral cortex. This is a signal of alarm and causes the brain to prepare the body for fight or flight.

Too much norepinephrine may cause aggressive behavior; however, inadequate levels of this chemical may cause an individual to seek thrills, which will then trigger the release of norepinephrine in the brain (Rupp, 1998). Career criminals have been found to have low levels of norepinephrine. They appear to lack displays of emotion or remorse (Kotulak, 1996). This neurotransmitter plays a role in attention and learning as well as being a memory enhancer. Vitamin C is critical to the synthesis of this chemical (Amen, 2005).

Oxytocin

Recent research suggests that oxytocin is an important chemical related to the stress response in females. It has been stated that women resist the fight-or-flight response and instead they "tend and befriend." Oxytocin is released for bonding purposes when a mother gives birth or when someone falls in love. It is important as educators that we realize the needs of our female students and allow them to talk things over when they experience stress (Taylor et al., 2000).

Serotonin

This neurotransmitter has been associated with many problems. It has been linked to depression, migraines, premenstrual syndrome, attention deficit disorder (ADD), obsessive-compulsive disorder, and aggressive and violent behavior (Niehoff, 1999). **Serotonin** is produced in the brain stem and is distributed throughout the brain, especially in the emotional areas. It helps cells communicate smoothly; their transmission becomes effortless with the appropriate amount of serotonin. Too little of this chemical is associated with obsessive-compulsive disorder, impulsivity, and overactivity in the anterior cingulate, the part of the brain that helps us focus. In general, individuals will get stuck on specific thoughts and be unable to refocus. It is also associated with depression and sometimes violence (Amen, 2005).

There is a bright side to serotonin. It is necessary for a sense of calm and well-being. Positive feedback has been suggested as a possible solution to low serotonin levels. In several studies, it was found that individuals with high self-esteem also had high levels of serotonin in their systems. They were found to be socially adept and happy people. Those with low self-esteem had low levels of the chemical, were unhappy, and had difficulty handling relationships. In extreme cases, these students were impulsive, aggressive, and sometimes violent (Sylwester, 1997b). After receiving positive feedback, some students with lower serotonin levels not only raised those levels but also began getting along with others.

Serotonin helps convey messages.

Critical cases could lead to depression or violence that would probably need to be controlled with medication. Antidepressants are often used successfully because they allow more serotonin to flow freely in the necessary areas of the brain.

The Importance of Neurotransmitters

The aid that neurotransmitters give messages allows for clearer thinking. It is especially important in the communication between the limbic system's amygdala and the prefrontal cortex. The prefrontal cortex helps the amygdala regulate its responses (Goleman, 1998b). The combinations and perfect balance of these chemicals affect and are affected by every thought, every word, and every action. Norepinephrine, dopamine, and serotonin are vital to the message control in the cortex. Like air traffic controllers, they slow down some messages, speed up others, and help each transmission land safely so that appropriate action can take place. Too little of these chemicals will cause an inefficient system—too much, and chaos could ensue. These "Munchkins" keep the travel on the Yellow Brick Road moving along at a steady speed.

WE'RE OFF TO *BE* THE WIZARD

As we set off on this journey, knowledge of the brain will aid our understanding of the learning process. Since learning changes the brain, we hope to change it on a daily basis. Using research-based strategies that have been tried and found successful in my classroom and in many others, I hope you are able to make the connections between how the brain learns and what your students need. Some of them are dealing with stress on a regular and sometimes dangerous level. Others are trying to deal with their emotions and with relationships with family members and peers. We still have those students who have come to school because they understand the importance of an education and are encouraged in their homes to do well.

By understanding the brain and its development, we can meet the needs of our students: physical needs, emotional and social needs, and cognitive needs. We can be aware of what nourishes their brains literally and figuratively. As we travel the Yellow Brick Road, we will find strategies to lower stress, handle emotions, raise achievement and levels of thinking, deal with students who have different brains, manage the classroom, and make the journey easier, more exciting, and stimulating for all of our students. Let's go down the road a bit farther and see where it takes us.

We're Off to See . . .

Beginning with the end in mind, we will approach the learning environment and our goals, standards, and objectives. A brain-compatible environment begins with a clear understanding of its purpose. A safe physical, emotional, and cognitive atmosphere includes the feedback necessary for the brain to orient itself to the learning.

WIZDOM

Key Points to Ponder

1. The brain seeks chemical balance, and what happens in the classroom can affect that balance.

2. The frontal lobe that deals with planning and decision making is the last to mature.

3. As research continues, scientists will offer us additional information.

Suggestions

Information on the brain is growing at a rapid pace. As educators, we must keep ourselves current as new discoveries are made. Become familiar with credible sources for current research. The following Web sites may be helpful:

- http://www.aan.com. American Academy of Neurology
- http://www.dana.org. Dana Alliance for Brain Initiatives
- http://www.sfn.org. Society for Neuroscience
- http://www.brainconnection.com. Brain Connection

3 No Place Like Home

No matter how dreary and gray our homes are, we people of flesh and blood would rather live there than in any other country, be it ever so beautiful. There is no place like home.

—Dorothy

Spring is in the air: Birds are singing, and flowers are blooming. It is Day 4 of a school review for the state board of education. Along with a team of reviewers, I am exhausted from observing teachers, interviewing students, teachers, and parents, and also shadowing students.

The school is neat and organized. The teachers are warm and friendly. They are without a doubt devoted to their jobs and to the children. Their unwritten mission statement appears to be "Whatever these children need, we will provide it."

The problem as I see it is that they don't understand the brain. The goal of the faculty is to have perfect discipline. They use a behavioral model. To offset the negative consequences, extrinsic motivation in the form of candy is extensively used. I watch as students lower their hands for a question when they realize they have received all the candy they are going to get. Why bother thinking anymore? The children walk the halls like little robots.

I sigh as I see how far this school has come and how far it needs to go. The students sit in groups, yet they do no group work. Teachers stand and deliver for 30 to 45 minutes, expecting all students to sit quietly. A lot of teaching is going on, but I wonder how much learning is actually taking place.

AN EMOTIONAL LEARNING ENVIRONMENT

Home is defined as an environment offering security and happiness, a valued place regarded as a refuge. If we want our classrooms to be places where students feel good about themselves and learn, we must create an environment for learning that affords a "there's no place like home" feeling. For some of our students, our classrooms are the safest refuge they have. It is often with us, their teachers, that they can feel free enough to experience safety and happiness. It is through this secure feeling that the brain is allowed to access higher levels of functioning, where real learning can take place. Yet, many educators today are still under the misguided impression that students who sit quietly are the ones doing the learning. They seem to think that the teacher stands at the front of the room and pours out pearls of wisdom that are somehow going straight into those little heads in the classroom, and if the students don't open their mouths, none of it will spill out!

The behavioral model that the school in the opening scenario uses encourages extrinsic rewards. Alfie Kohn has been writing about the negative effects of reward systems for years. Rewards especially have a tendency to put kids in a box. If this is what the teacher wants for an A, for a candy bar, or for a soda, that is exactly what he or she gets. There is no sense in taking a risk and trying something new! I found that students who were less academically oriented often gave up when I offered rewards. Kohn explains how this threatens such students. If I offer a reward for something they don't feel capable of doing, then I am really threatening not to give them one unless they can do what the other kids are doing (Kohn, 1993).

Students want to feel emotional connection and academic success.

What about testing? State-standardized testing is putting a strain on the classroom. Teachers have little time for interaction with their students. The necessary feedback is often forgotten, because information must be covered in time for the test. Students are feeling the pressure and want someone to talk to about it. The teachers are too busy to discuss anything other than content. Content is not what is on the minds and in the hearts of most students (Oliveira, 1999).

What I will describe in this book are strategies for creating a brain-friendly environment. Understanding and honoring brain function, learning styles, states, music, rapport, and memory pathways help kids feel at home. It builds trust in you as their teacher and coach. If you create this kind of atmosphere, students will feel safe and understood. But that isn't enough. Students want to feel academic success. So, the first step in brain-based teaching is making the brain-centered classroom one in which all students feel successful. To promote long-term memories, self-confidence, and a love of learning, let's look at an enriched environment.

WHAT ARE ENRICHED ENVIRONMENTS?

Neuroscientists have been talking about the concept of enriched environments for many years. One way that learning affects the brain is seen in changes at the cellular level. Dr. Marian Diamond, of the University of California, Berkeley, and Dr. William Greenough, of the University of Illinois, have done extensive work on enrichment. They have both spent years studying the brain growth of rats in different environments. These studies have offered interesting ideas to the field of education. We do not want to compare our students to rats, but comparing brain growth and composition is worthwhile.

Many of the studies have dealt with the idea of enriched environments and impoverished environments. In one such study (Barber, Barrett, Beals, Bergman, & Diamond, 1999), the control group consisted of lab rats in their normal lab environment: three rats in a small cage with food and water. Experimental groups consisted of isolated rats, rats with companions, and rats with companions in a large environment, with toys representing challenge. The challenges were running wheels, tubes, blocks, and bars.

The results of the experiment are interesting. The control group, three rats in a small cage with no toys, showed more brain growth than a single rat in a small cage with no toys. It appeared that socialization helped brains grow. A single rat in a large cage with toys fared better than a single rat with no toys. Challenges seemed to support growth. However, the three rats without toys did better than a single rat with toys; hence it appeared that socialization promoted more learning than toys did. Social life encourages challenges, such as problem solving. Calculations have to be made about behavior and its consequences (Calvin, 1996). The twelve rats in a large cage with toys showed the most growth. The enriched environment encouraged wide branching of brain cells. One of the more interesting observations from this study was the comparison of twelve rats with no toys with a group of three rats with no toys. Which of them showed more growth? Did more socialization cause more learning to take place? The answer was "no." The three rats showed more growth than the twelve rats. Perhaps too much socialization caused stress. Perhaps this was a case in which individualized attention made a difference.

Does this experiment and others like it prove that rats that grew and developed in enriched environments are smarter? We know they have more connections and cortical thickness, but are they brighter than other rats? The answer is "yes." Those rats remembered how to find the cheese in a maze after just one learning session. The important point is that with the proper environment, brain growth can be seen, and with poor environments, the shrinkage of brain cells can also be seen (Diamond & Hopson, 1998).

Both challenge and feedback are required for brain growth.

Dr. Greenough's similar research suggests that two things are necessary for brain growth through enrichment. The first is that the subject must be challenged, and the second is that the subject must receive feedback. Novelty may be included in the challenge but is not always necessary; however, timely feedback is necessary for learning to take place (Jensen, 2005).

What About Humans?

Autopsy studies have compared the brains of high school dropouts with the brains of graduate students. From those studies, it was determined that the graduate students had more brain growth—up to 25 percent more—than the dropouts. The critical component of this growth was a continually challenging environment (Jensen, 2000a).

Of course, there are the now-famous nun studies conducted by Dr. David Snowdon (2001). These women from Mankato, Minnesota, whose longevity was astounding to the neuroscientist, donated their brains to his research group. His scientific interest in them concerned not only their extended lives but also their energy and intellectual capabilities well into advanced age. There was certainly some forgetfulness, but most of the nuns remained active and able to perform complex cognitive skills until the end of their lives. Because these women were so mentally active, they had brains rich with connections. As a result, even some with Alzheimer's disease showed little outward evidence of the brain deterioration associated with the disease. It seems that the more active and challenging your life remains, the more connections you can afford to lose!

The resiliency experts agree that to produce appropriate developmental outcomes, a nurturing environment that meets the need for belonging, competence, autonomy, and safety is necessary.

Jensen insists that enrichment begins with contrast (2005). If what we offer at school is not different from what the students have in their other environments, then we are not truly enriching them.

CAN WE PROVIDE AN ENRICHED ENVIRONMENT IN THE CLASSROOM?

The resiliency experts agree that to produce appropriate developmental outcomes, a nurturing environment that meets the need for belonging, competence, autonomy, and safety is necessary. Meeting these needs will lead to a sense of hope. The guidelines include an environment that includes caring relationships, high expectations, and opportunities for participation and contribution (Benard, 2004). As I mentioned in the first chapter, these are helpful for children in any economic group.

For you Wizard of Oz fans, these three guidelines can be applied to the metaphor. First, the Cowardly Lion needs caring relationships to lower his stress, which will allow him to learn. Next, the Tin Man would love to participate and feel like he is participating. And finally, the Scarecrow would expect nothing less than high expectations. We want to challenge students and promote brain growth as well as provide a safe environment in which we can encourage self-confidence and a love of learning. We know we need to help our students meet our state standards, and we want to keep stress levels—theirs and ours—as low as possible. Academic failure is one cause of the stress we see in our classrooms. Stress causes social and behavioral problems as well as depression in children (Tallal, 1999).

Neuroscientist Paula Tallal (1999) speaks of enrichment in the classroom. The following learning principles, based on neuroscience research, can be used to make changes in the brain:

1. Give the brain something it is able to do.

2. Provide repetition to get neurons firing repeatedly and to enable them to become more efficient at firing for that information.

3. Give timely feedback, either positive or negative.

4. Adapt the learning to each child. (Technology may be helpful in the differentiation process: It can track performance and give immediate feedback.)

5. Consistency and intensity are important; don't be afraid to repeat!

Brains need time. To digest and adapt new information, the brain needs both time and opportunity (Diamond, 1999a). One thing that appeals to the brain is novelty. This appeal may be the result of the brain dealing with survival. Something new and different must be examined to make sure it is not harmful (Carper, 2000). Research on the adolescent brain suggests that using novelty is one of the few approaches that is effective in reaching the middle and high school student (Feinstein, 2004). Indeed, because the brain habituates so easily to the common, everyday occurrences, it is little wonder that we all, in general, are attracted to the unusual.

As a classroom teacher, I have felt the pressure of standardized-test time. Test preparation seemed to begin earlier each year. In some classrooms, the entire curriculum is dropped for months, as teachers prepare students for the tests. Education revolves around them. It is so natural for all of us to fall back into our old routines and teach the same old way. It appears a faster way to cover all the material before the test. Hence the question, "Can I create a brain-compatible classroom, enrich the environment, and further the learning my students must have for our standardized tests?"

Predictability, novelty, control, choice, challenge, feedback, and success help build resiliency.

As I look at the components of an enriched classroom environment, as well as what our students need to become resilient, I can focus on the following requirements: *predictability, novelty, control, choice, challenge, feedback,* and *success.* Can we provide these requirements in this atmosphere of high-stakes accountability?

An Environment for Success

I believe strongly that every child wants to succeed. Success is part of what makes the classroom a safe place for many of our students. Our assessment techniques inform our students, parents, administrators, and community members of the success of our students and our schools. The journey through school has been a difficult one for those who have had a sense of failure in the assessment arena.

In recent years, I have taken a new approach to accountability and assessment. In studying the work of Stiggins, Arter, Chappuis, and Chappuis (2005), Wiggins and McTighe (2005), and Jacobs (2004), I have devised my own formula for teachers to use when dealing with teaching to standards, goals, objectives, or even school curricula. I call it *Ready? Aim. Fire!* It uses backward design, learning targets, and matching assessments.

Ready?

The brain needs to know what it needs to know. This is part of what predictability embraces. Getting ready indicates that both the teacher and the students are clear about what it is they need to know. This requires what Rick Stiggins and others (2005) call "clear targets." Take your standard, objective, performance descriptor, benchmark, or whatever you use to guide your teaching, and create these targets. Targets can be defined as exactly what you expect your students to learn and be able to communicate to you through the assessment that you are going to give. If you align your assessments, units, and lessons to these targets, the focus should be pretty clear.

Think of an archery target like that in Figure 3.1. The outer rim would be the Goal, the next would be the Standard, then the Benchmark, and finally the

Figure 3.1   Ready! Find the Bull's-Eye

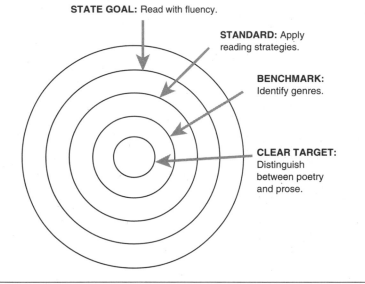

STATE GOAL: Read with fluency.

STANDARD: Apply reading strategies.

BENCHMARK: Identify genres.

CLEAR TARGET: Distinguish between poetry and prose.

NOTE: Reduce the big picture to clear, measurable targets. Specify exactly what you want your students to know.

Target: what you want your students to know. Write the target on the board or put it on a bulletin board. Create visual targets for students who will pay closer attention and focus more on those. If students ask you why they are doing something, point to that target. If your students cannot make the connection between what they are currently doing in the classroom and that target, perhaps it's time to reconsider what you have planned.

This is all part of backward design. This process takes us from our large goals and centers us on our smaller goals. This is the first step in the process.

Aim

Once you know what you expect your students to know, produce, or perform, it is time to determine what kind of assessment will give you that information. Will a paper-and-pencil test give you the information you need and the feedback the students need? Are you able to do this in a selected-response format, or will it require essay questions? These are the kinds of questions you must ask yourself. The focus and the method must match.

Giving the brain meaning includes providing the necessary connection between what students are expected to know and how they are to meet those expectations. What are you aiming for? In the example in Figure 3.2, the target is to distinguish between poetry and prose. Assessment should be created that will allow students to show that they know the difference between the two genres. Perhaps the assessment would be to provide excerpts from each genre and asking students to write what type each excerpt is. With that in mind, the next step is

Fire!

Now it is time to plan your lessons. You have the target and the assessment to guide you. Your instruction now must match the two. Creating lesson plans is something we probably do best. However, before we understood the importance of making this match, we sometimes would go off in different directions instead of staying focused. A possible lesson plan for this target is in Figure 3.2.

Figure 3.2   After Creating a Clear Goal or Target, Create the Assessment, and Then Design the Lesson

Goal: Read with fluency.

Standard: Apply reading strategies.

Benchmark: Identify different genres.

Target: Distinguish between poetry and prose.

Ready?	Aim	Fire!
Distinguish between poetry and prose.	Assessment: Students will read several selections and determine whether each is prose or poetry.	1. Discuss the organization of prose: paragraphs, sentences, etc. 2. Read several poems and discuss their organization: stanzas, verses, etc. 3. Ask students to find both prose and poetry on the same or similar topics.
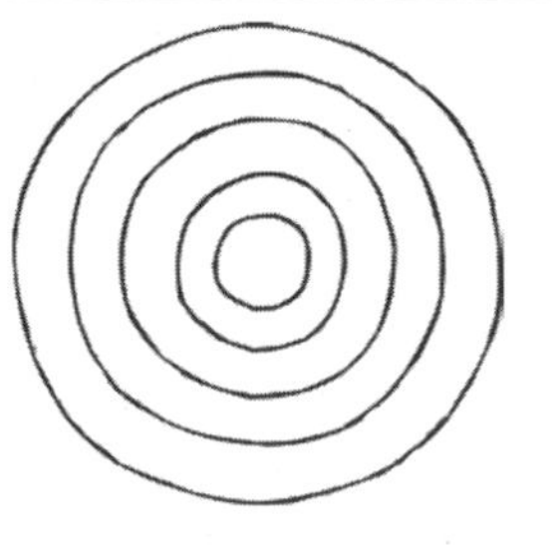	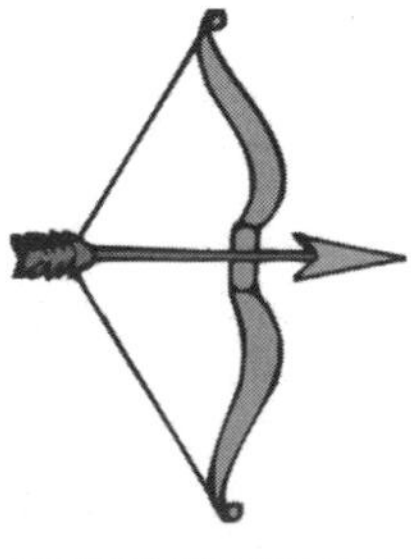	

AN ENVIRONMENT WHERE ASSESSMENT IS ENRICHMENT

Let's face it. Although we want to put our students as our first priority, sometimes summative assessments, like our state tests, are put first. Assessment is more than summative. In fact, formative assessments provide the information students need to consistently succeed. So, can we provide assessment with predictability, choice, challenge, control, and feedback to make our students more resilient in the testing process?

Is Assessment Predictable?

We have defined predictability as the quality of knowing what is going to happen. It gives students an internal locus of control to have this information. Can we make assessment predictable?

First of all, ongoing assessment should be predictable. Students should know that as you teach the lesson or unit, you will be assessing their knowledge. It can be as easy as 1, 2, 3 (see Figure 3.3). Asking students to raise their hands every time you ask a question will get them in the habit of attending to what you are

> We have defined predictability as the quality of knowing what is going to happen. It gives students an internal locus of control to have this information.

saying, participating, and self-assessing. Also, for some students who never raise their hands due to lack of confidence or knowledge, this will be an opportunity. Telling them to have one finger raised if they know the answer and you can call on them, two fingers if they think they might know and you can call on them if you are desperate, or three fingers if they don't know and don't wish to be called on provides you with a great deal of information. This very informal assessment allows you to divide the class into three groups and provide appropriate material according to their readiness; Depending on the assessment, you can either reteach the whole class or move on to more challenging material. This also allows you to build trust as you call only on those with the appropriate signal.

A variation of this is the All Thumbs strategy: thumbs up, thumbs down, and thumbs sideways. Some teachers prefer to use this for older students. The premise is the same, but the signals are different: thumbs up if you know it, thumbs sideways if you're not sure, and thumbs down if you are having difficulty (see Figure 3.4).

Let's talk about pop quizzes. I have researched these in the past few years. I had always been afraid that they would overwhelm students and cause the stress response, so I did not recommend them. From my research, I have

Figure 3.3   Hands in the Air Strategy for Quick Assessment

Raising hand with 1 finger	I know it. You can call on me.	
Raising hand with 2 fingers	I might know it. Call on me if no one else knows.	
Raising hand with 3 fingers	Nope. I don't know it. I trust you not to call on me.	

Figure 3.4   All Thumbs Strategy to Assess Whole Group

Thumb up	I know it. You can call on me.	
Thumb sideways	I might know it. Call on me if no one else knows.	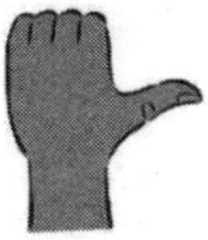
Thumb down	Nope. I don't know it. I trust you not to call on me.	

discovered the value of unannounced quizzes and tests. They actually do help raise achievement test scores (Graham, 1999). The reason: You are assessing long-term memory as opposed to working memory. When we announce a test or quiz, our students study right before the test, and often we discover only what they have learned in the last few minutes or hours. A teacher in one of my graduate classes gave me the answer to my dilemma. From the beginning of the year, he tells the students that they must be prepared for unannounced quizzes on any day. In this way, the quizzes became part of the routine and were more predictable.

Another way to make assessment more predictable and brain-compatible is to use practice tests. Standardized test-preparation manuals are available to make students comfortable with the format and style. Testing research tells us that students must be taught test-prep skills every year, as the skills tend not to stay in long-term memory, and because achievement tests change (Casanova & Berliner, 1986).

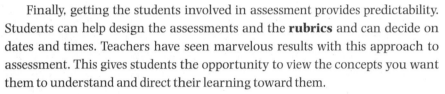

> Another way to make assessment more predictable and brain-compatible is to use practice tests.

Finally, getting the students involved in assessment provides predictability. Students can help design the assessments and the **rubrics** and can decide on dates and times. Teachers have seen marvelous results with this approach to assessment. This gives students the opportunity to view the concepts you want them to understand and direct their learning toward them.

Can We Offer Choice with Assessment?

Choice is a strong component of enrichment. Making choices involves problem solving. This encourages the brain to search for patterns and connect the new material to the previously stored material. The blood flow to the neural connections stimulates dendritic growth (Fogarty, 2001).

Giving students choices in their assessments adds to their internal feeling of control. They may be able to assure their success when they choose their assessment. This can be done in a number of ways. Perhaps some units would free you to offer a traditional paper-and-pencil test, a creative project, a written paper, or an oral presentation.

Should Assessments Provide Novelty?

Is it possible to be predictable and novel at the same time? Absolutely. The novelty may come with the assessment choices. It may come in a creative form, such as directing the students to create a new kind of test that has never been given and will accurately assess the concepts you are working on. Perhaps they will be able to extrapolate the learning to the real world using novel approaches. This enables more memory pathways to be used and thus enables the brain to offer greater access to the information beyond the assessment time.

Novelty can certainly be offered in the form of **performance assessment.** Creating videos, hypermedia presentations, puppet shows, interviews, surveys, or graphic organizers may pique the brain's attention and encourage curiosity and risk-taking.

Here is a note of caution: Too much novelty causes stress and brain shrinkage in lab animals. Stress is known to kill brain cells in the hippocampus, the structure associated with factual memory. Even though we are aware of the need for novelty with adolescents, use caution. Their decision-making skills are still developing. Make a commitment to guide your students in novel situations.

Should Assessments Always Be Challenging?

The importance of challenge cannot be understated. Diamond (1999a) suggests an appropriate amount of challenge. If a situation is too challenging, students will be overwhelmed. What constitutes challenge? Going back to the steps outlined by Tallal (1999), a challenge would appear at the adaptation stage. Challenge brings with it the feeling of capability. Intrinsic motivation is usually involved: "I know how to do it; I'm interested in doing it; I can do it!" A suitable challenge would involve only positive stress.

Challenges may include many levels of the new Bloom's Taxonomy (Anderson et al., 2001; see Figure 3.5). Remembering, understanding, applying, analyzing, evaluating, and creating can be incorporated into problem solving, decision making, explanations, planning, representation, and prediction

Figure 3.5   The Cognitive Dimension of the Bloom's Revised Taxonomy

The Knowledge Dimension	Remember	Understand	Apply	Analyze	Evaluate	Create
Factual	Identify the terms.	Prepare a flow chart.	Make up a puzzle or game.	Write a biography.	Prepare a list of criteria.	Write a commercial.
Conceptual	Identify similarities and differences.	Write a summary.	Take photos to illustrate a point.	Conduct an investigation.	Conduct a debate.	Sell an idea.
Procedural	Explain the method.	Create a cartoon strip.	Construct a model.	Make a family tree.	Make a booklet of important information.	Create a new product.
Meta-cognitive	Describe your thoughts.	Describe how you interpret the theme.	Design a marketing strategy.	Design questions you would want answered.	Choose a panel to discuss views.	Make up a new language.

Figure 3.6 Some Optional Approaches to Working With the New Bloom

- All children work through the remembering and understanding stages and then select at least one activity from each other level.
- All children work through first two levels and then select activities from any other level.
- Some students work at lower levels while others work at higher levels.
- Students select activities from any level.
- Some activities are tagged "must do" while others are "may do."
- One thinking process is selected for all students to use; for example, students work in small groups or individually to identify similarities and differences.
- Some students work through the lower levels using the teacher's activities and then design their own activities at the higher levels while other students may be ready to design their own activities at all levels.
- All students write their own activities from the taxonomy.

(Perkins, 1995). Can these be assessed? They can definitely be included in both traditional paper-and-pencil tests and **authentic assessment.**

Figure 3.6 shows how you might use the taxonomy in your classroom. (We will revisit the new Bloom in relation to higher level thinking and multiple intelligences in Chapter 6.) The concept of self-esteem includes the ability to confront challenges and learn from the experiences (Brooks, 1999). Isn't that what we want for all our students?

Even in the studies of rats, brain growth varied according to the kind of challenge. Rats running on wheels showed some new growth and branching, but rats that did more acrobatic feats, such as crawling along a raised pole, showed more growth (Jensen, 2000a).

Assessment Is Feedback

This would be the foundation of an enriched environment. Assessment would be feedback rather than a simple determination of success or failure. If we want all our students to succeed by meeting the standards, we must give them continual feedback. Assessment should be viewed as an opportunity to communicate the current level of performance and provide information to enhance that performance. By furnishing students with explicit information regarding their current status in terms of objectives, achievement has been reported to have increased 37 percent. Feedback is considered to be the most important ingredient to enhance achievement (Marzano, 2000).

> Feedback is considered to be the most important ingredient to enhance achievement.

If we truly want our students involved in the learning process, they must have the information they need to continue their search for knowledge. Any kind of assessment is an opportunity to give and receive feedback. In a study done with graduate students, those who were given no feedback on a problem-solving simulation lost as much self-confidence as the students who received negative feedback (Goleman, 1998b).

Assessment Offers a Feeling of Control

I saved this for last, because assessment offers our students a feeling of control if we have provided predictability, challenge, choice, and feedback. If students become involved in assessment, they will feel some control over their education and responsibility for their learning. They will accept the idea that their ability determines academic success. Learning challenges and risk-taking are no longer stressful, as students face them knowing that they are able to achieve (Stiggins et al., 2005).

The new social studies textbooks arrive with all the fancy trimmings: publisher tests, educational software, posters, audiotapes, and DVDs—more than the teacher, Geri, can imagine getting through. The curriculum seems wonderful; she can't wait to get started. She begins using the text, showing some clips, and having her students listen to some of the tapes.

There is so much material for her to learn and to share with her students that she doesn't appreciate how much time is passing. She suddenly realizes that it is time to move on to another unit. But first, how will she assess her students? Because this great program has tests included, she decides to give her students the publisher's test for the unit.

It is very disappointing when most of the class fails. What is the matter with these students? She rethinks the entire situation. She covered the material in a predictable fashion. Geri enjoys using the memory research for her units, so she had been sure to apply that.

The day she passes back the tests, she is very frustrated. She asks the students what they think might be the problem. One student replies, "Mrs. B.," as they call her, "that test didn't ask what we learned." "Yeah," says another, "I'm not sure what memory pathway that test information was supposed to be stored in, but it wasn't in any of mine!" Geri laughs at this, but it makes her think. Had she taught the students in such a way that memories were not stored where they were needed? That was a possibility, but there was more. The publisher's test didn't really cover the material she thought was the most important! The assessment and the instruction just didn't match.

The following day, Geri asks her students to work in teams to create criteria for assessing the unit. What would a student who truly understood the material, enough for a grade of A, have to know? After sharing these lists with the whole class and determining A criteria, she asks them to create criteria for the other possible grades. When all groups finish, they compare notes. Some argue about a few points, but eventually the entire class reaches a consensus.

The next day, Geri asks each team to create an assessment. They may choose to create a fact-recognition test, an essay test, or a performance assessment. For either of the latter two, they must create a rubric. It takes her students three class periods to create assessments that satisfy the original standards the class had created.

Then, she offers them a choice of assessments, with the caveat that no student may use the assessment that he or she designed. Because of the hard work they had put into creating the standards and their own assessments, the students score well. Enabling them to choose gives them the power to express their knowledge in the format they think will work best for them. Self-confidence is high, because the students know that they know the material.

Geri realized that the book test had not sought the information she had covered. From then on, matching the instruction to the assessment became a priority. She also realized how empowering it was to share the assessment process with her students. They gained confidence in themselves through the experience. They would often ask to help her set the standards for other learning.

BRAIN-BASED ASSESSMENT

The most common types of assessment in use are traditional selected-response tests, essay tests, authentic or performance assessments, and **portfolios.** Report card grades and conferences are also assessments. Are all of these methods brain compatible? They can be. At issue here is the locus of control. Remember, this is one of your students' basic needs.

I am applying for a graduate program. To be accepted, I must take and score well on the Miller Analogies Test. I haven't been tested on anything in years, and it makes me a bit nervous. I go to the college bookstore and purchase a practice book for the test. It contains dozens of practice exams along with an explanation of how the analogies should be approached. I spend weeks preparing. I take many of the practice tests, finding some of them easy and others quite difficult.

On the day of the exam, I must drive to a nearby city to take the test at a state university. I am in a strange city, in a strange building, and in a strange room. So much for **episodic memory!** I am told the amount of time I will have to complete the exam. I am also told to use the restroom or get a drink before I begin, because I will not be allowed either until I finish. The exams are distributed, and I begin. It takes me several minutes to get comfortable in the room, but as I look over the test, I realize that I've practiced this format enough to feel in control. There are even a few analogies that were in the practice book! I forget about the time constraints and complete the exam with time to spare.

I was able to relax and do quite well on the test because the experience was predictable; I knew what the exam would be like. I had some control over the situation. The brain-antagonistic parts of the experience—the strange place and the time limits—were overcome by my self-confidence in the format and the material. I often carry with me a cartoon of a child showing his test paper to his dad. He says, "But Dad, I knew the answers to the questions that weren't on the test!"

Balance

I believe strongly that all the assessment methods when used appropriately have merit. Students must be able to handle all types, and each provides impor-

 Use many kinds of assessment for balance.

tant feedback. Although it is not very "in" to have students memorizing a lot of material, it is still very necessary for them to have a knowledge foundation to problem-solve, reason, compare, evaluate, and create. Processes and products are the result of thinking with content. To assess that knowledge foundation, paper-and-pencil tests work well.

If your focus is to have students speak persuasively, a paper-and-pencil test is not the method to use. It is possible to give students a written test on the parts of a speech, the reasons for support and details, and the merits of the different persuasive formats. To assess their speaking ability, they must perform. The criteria must be carefully selected either by you alone or with your students. Either way, the students must understand the criteria and have that in their hands when they are given the performance task. This will keep them focused, give them a feeling of control, and provide the predictability they need.

To keep assessment balanced, consider the following assessment options:

Paper-and-Pencil Recognition Tests

These include multiple choice, matching, true/false, and fill-in-the-blank tests. Don't underestimate these tests. They are not simply for factual knowledge. If they are created correctly, they can also assess reasoning and problem-solving. Recognition tests are efficient and effective when created well. There are guidelines for creating these items.

Recall or Essay Tests

These can be used in a variety of situations. Criteria must be decided on beforehand. If you are assessing application or reasoning rather than content knowledge, provide the content or give the essay questions to the students to study. Often, students can apply or reason, but they haven't mastered the content. This gives them the opportunity for valid assessment of the focus.

Authentic or Performance Assessment

These are opportunities for our students to show their abilities and knowledge through a product or performance. *Authentic assessment* is considered to be a task that might be encountered in the real world. *Performance assessment* does not have to meet this requirement. Some researchers call both tasks performance assessment, because the distinction is unclear (Marzano, 2000). This may be an opportunity for students to see the connection between school and the real world. It requires solid criteria. Authentic assessment can offer challenge, novelty, and choice. Because we have such diversity in the classroom, performance assessment affords students the freedom to create or perform in ways that are compatible with their learning styles or strong intelligences.

Portfolio Assessment

This collection of student work can have many purposes. As students collect their work, they can see their own growth and reflect on their learning. Portfolios can contain different types of materials, such as videotapes, audio-cassette tapes, essays, short stories, poetry, research papers, and tests. In a brain-based classroom, students are encouraged to put some appropriate personal items in their portfolios. When I share my portfolio with audiences, I always pull out a picture of my best products: my children. Students often want to personalize their portfolios with pictures of pets or other items they care about. This brings an emotional hook to the process.

Rubrics, checklists, and personal notes can be used to assess the items in a portfolio. Occasionally, teachers give portfolio grades, because they believe this will motivate students. Be careful with this, because the grade may be seen as a reward or punishment and affect the student's self-confidence. If you must grade it, be sure that students have the criteria as they are assembling their portfolios, or perhaps suggest that students pick the item or items they want graded.

Grades/Report Cards

This form of assessment is what tends to put students in a stressful state or in a box. Instead of enjoyment, the goal of learning becomes "What must I do to get an A." Thomas Armstrong believes this is a way to keep students from becoming the geniuses that they are. Comparisons are made, and sometimes competition begins (Armstrong, 1998).

Because we probably aren't going to eradicate report cards, let's find the best possible way to live with them. If our other forms of assessment are ongoing and offer continual feedback, report card grades should be a consensus of those assessments. When the focus of the learning and the methods of assessment match, students will be able to see what they are accomplishing and what they have yet to do.

Conferences

These are usually parent-teacher conferences, and I always feel that the biggest mistake we make is not including the person who has the most at stake—the student! Instead of talking about them, we should be talking with them. Rick Stiggins and colleagues' (2005) model of student-led conferences is one to be considered. This format gives students the responsibility for their achievement. There are numerous other benefits, such as improved student-teacher and student-parent relations.

Student-teacher conferences are very powerful ways of giving and receiving feedback. For the continuous feedback that is necessary for a brain-compatible classroom, the teacher cannot be the only source. It is important to use your teams and other configurations of students for this purpose; however, it is also very important that teachers meet one-on-one with students for brief conferencing. Sometimes, just brief meetings can promote higher achievement.

HOME SWEET HOME

Research suggests that the more collaboration between teacher and student on the goals of learning and performance, the better the learning environment.

> Research suggests that the more collaboration between teacher and student on the goals of learning and performance, the better the learning environment.

Teachers who highlight the importance of using strategies for learning and memory as well as the importance of putting forth effort are helping students gain control over their learning (Holloway, 2000). The students are the most important component. We can spend a lot of time teaching, but if our students do not want to learn, they won't.

Creating an atmosphere that makes all students feel safe sounds like a tall order. But I hope you will see from the chapters that follow that it is possible. When we meet the needs of our students by giving them control and responsibility over their learning and by offering them novelty, predictability, choice, challenge, and feedback, we are giving them the opportunity to understand how they learn best.

The futurists predict that our students will be living up to 150 years. Considering all the breakthroughs in genetic research, I believe this is possible. My two children have careers that weren't available 10 years ago. We are preparing our students for a world we know nothing about. If we are truly effective educators, our students will leave us with the skills to remain lifelong learners.

> We are working on infomercials for our state unit. The student teams are at various levels of accomplishing the task. One of the teams is working on a computer presentation. Another is videotaping one of its segments. The social studies teacher and I work together to help the students learn to communicate information in a variety of ways.
>
> As I dash from team to team handing out observation notes on their teamwork, I pass by Jay. Without looking up from the computer keyboard, he says, "Is this okay, Mom?" I turn. Jay realizes his error. His face is red, and the students are trying to control their laughter. He mumbles, "I didn't mean to say that. Come on, you guys!" To give him time to recover, I say, "Hasn't that ever happened to the rest of you? You get really comfortable somewhere and you're enjoying what you're doing—and you sort of forget where you are?" The kids nod and go back to their work. I go over to Jay to see what he wants. Because Jay has been one of my greatest challenges, I decide that I am flattered.
>
> "How can I help you, Jay?"
>
> "I can't even remember, but you know, I was having so much fun making this poster for our video, I thought I was home!"

We're Off to See . . .

Now that we understand the need for clear targets, we will continue down the Yellow Brick Road. First, we will encounter the Cowardly Lion and strategies to lower stress in the classroom.

WIZDOM

Key Points to Ponder

1. Assessment provides feedback that helps the brain know what it needs to learn and remember.

2. Assessment can be enriching to the brain when it offers choice, challenge, and novelty.

3. The more involved students are with assessment, the more ownership they will take with the learning.

Suggestions

- There are excellent resources on authentic assessment: *How to Assess Authentic Learning,* by Kay Burke (2000), and the work of Rick Stiggins et al. (2005) on assessment are enlightening.
- Be cautious about giving students credit or extrinsic rewards for poor or inadequate work to raise self-esteem. There is a concept called *learned laziness* in which subjects are rewarded no matter what they do. As a result, they feel they have no control over their own actions (Sapolsky, 2004).
- Consider asking students to personalize their learning space to make your room more comfortable and more like home.

4 If I Only Had the Nerve

Dealing With Stress

"But that isn't right. The King of Beasts shouldn't be a coward," said the Scarecrow.

"I know it," returned the Lion, wiping a tear from his eye with the tip of his tail. "It is my great sorrow and makes my life very unhappy. But whenever there is danger, my heart begins to beat fast."

"This is the worst day of my life!" Jana thinks as she waits at the bus stop. "My first day at a new school and I have to take the bus just like a kid. Why can't we live closer so I can walk? Or why can't Mom save enough money for a car? I'll be able to get my license next year, but what good is it going to do me? I'm going to get a job and save up for my own car. After school today, I'm going to start looking for something. I need something to do anyway, since I don't know anyone here." She gets on the bus and finds herself staring at dozens of unfamiliar faces. And they are staring back at her. Suddenly, her heart starts racing. "Where should I sit? Are there any empty seats? I guess I have to sit next to someone. I wonder if it's cool to sit in the front or if I should go to the back?" All of these thoughts race through her head as she plops down into a seat. She doesn't look at the person next to her. She knows it's a girl, but that's all. The sweat starts trickling down her arm and Jana wipes the perspiration from her forehead.

She stares at the back of the boy's head in front of her and prays that the ride will be over soon. Jana thinks everyone is looking at her. Her mouth is dry and she can barely swallow. As the bus pulls up in front of the school, Jana gathers her things together and practically pushes her way through the riders to get off the bus. She races into the building and frantically looks for the office, so she can get her schedule. Through the crowded halls she finds her way to her counselor, Mrs. Hines. When she knocks on the door, there is no answer. Jana leans against the wall as her tears begin to fall.

The symptoms of this brain/body response were Jana's racing heart, dry mouth, and the crying. The chemicals that were circulating in her brain helped take this memory from short-term to long-term storage. They *marked* this experience for her in such a way that several years later, she not only can recall the day, but doing so causes the same physical responses.

We all know what it's like to experience stress. It has become a negative word in our vocabulary since Dr. Hans Selye first coined it decades ago. Stress, however, is not necessarily a bad thing. Life would not be very exciting without a little stress in it. What we have commonly called stress covers several types of situations and has been defined by Selye as *a nonspecific response of the body to a demand* (Sapolsky, 2004). What is problematic about stress is that one person's biggest nightmare is another's greatest pleasure. For instance, my husband has a private pilot's license. Scott loves to fly small planes and does so for relaxation and fun. I, on the other hand, am as happy about flying with him as I would be about jumping off a very tall building! Needless to say, he flies without me. Scott experiences **eustress,** or positive stress, from flying, and I experience *distress*, or bad stress, from the same experience. Sometimes it is difficult to determine the difference between the two.

The excitement that you feel before a first date and the nervousness at a job interview are examples of the positive stress response, or eustress. Our response system was designed to keep us alive. It was intended to get our bodies prepared to flee or fight. At this milder level, it simply keeps us on our toes. Some of us experience this response when we go to the dentist. Because these experiences in our lives are intermittent and random, they do not cause us to be in the state of stress or distress in which the Cowardly Lion lived. I like to say that anyone in this constant distressed state "has his or her alarm button on."

> Our response system was designed to keep us alive. It was intended to get our bodies prepared to flee or fight.

Sally is a sixth grader in my language arts class. A very delightful child, she has a smile on her face most of the time. She has a nice circle of friends, participates in basketball, and takes piano lessons. Sally's parents are volunteers at school whenever they can be away from their jobs. Sally's dad works for a large company and may be transferred at any time. Her mother is a secretary at their church.

Sally begins to miss school occasionally. She returns with dark circles under her eyes. Makeup work is difficult for her to complete, and her grades begin to suffer. She begins to miss more school, and her parents call for a conference. Rather than talk about her illness, they want to know only how she can bring up her grades. They say they will punish her and keep her off the basketball team if that is necessary. Alarmed, I encourage them to refrain from any form of punishment. Perhaps Sally can stay after school a few nights and make up her work. Mom and Dad leave still visibly upset.

More days are missed, and Sally returns looking tired. She is coughing and has great trouble controlling it. She is no longer socializing with her friends. They try to get her to go with them at recess and during gym, but she avoids them and spends some of her time in my classroom, just sitting. She doesn't speak, and I don't intrude on her privacy.

Friday is our writing workshop time. Today, we are going to do some creative writing. I turn on classical music that includes nature sounds. One of the students suggests that I turn off the lights while they visualize the scene, and I do so.

Sally gives an audible gasp, jumps out of her seat, and leaves the room. We have no counselor, so the principal and I retrieve the child from the bathroom and escort her to the office. She sits with a look of terror on her face. Eventually, weeks later, she reveals the horror of her abuse. The perpetrator is not either parent. He is a neighbor who follows her into the house after school. Some of her absences have been attempts to keep the house locked and the intruder out. The cough and other illnesses are the results of not sleeping as she tries to solve her problem and keep her parents happy. Her condition could also be aggravated by the suppression of her immune system from the stress.

Sally was living with her alarm button always on. The abuse she suffered changed her brain. She focused on protecting herself and became hypervigilant in doing so. She could no longer focus on school or her friends.

Studies have shown that abuse can cause reactions in children that are very different from those in nonabused children. This information can be noticed in the electrical activity in their brains and the chemical levels in their bloodstreams (Fauber, 1999). Abused children are at a higher risk for depression, suicide, and substance abuse (McEwen & Lasley, 2001).

Selye noticed the similarity in symptoms in stressful situations and called them the stress syndrome or the general adaptation syndrome (GAS). He distinguished three stages in this syndrome: *alarm, resistance,* and *exhaustion* (Sternberg, 2000).

A racing heart is only the beginning. Let's look at what this stress response does to the brain and the body. To understand this, you must look at the autonomic nervous system. It is divided into three more systems: the **sympathetic nervous system,** the **parasympathetic nervous system,** and the **enteric nervous system.** For my purposes, I will look at just the sympathetic and parasympathetic nervous systems. These two networks are important in situations that cause stress and also in nonemergency situations in which we can relax: These would be, respectively, the fight-or-flight circumstances and the *feed and read* conditions.

THE SYMPATHETIC NERVOUS SYSTEM

Audrey is a bully. Audrey was bullied at home. The only thing that makes Audrey feel good about herself is to have power over others. As a result, many of the second graders are afraid of her. She is twice the size of many of them. She calls them names. She threatens them. Once Audrey was seen "hurling" a student out of the classroom.

What is truly alarming about this situation is that Audrey is the teacher. It takes some time before anyone realizes what is going on in Room 103, Miss Audrey Brice's classroom. It begins with some students not wanting to go to school.

Every morning Carl's mother walks him to the bus stop. She gets up early with him and fixes him a healthy breakfast. She checks his book bag and makes sure he has his homework. On this particular Monday morning, Carl complains of a headache. His mother checks his forehead for fever and tells him that his headache will probably disappear by the time he gets to school. She is a bit concerned, as he has been complaining of headaches in recent days. As the bus arrives, Carl starts to shiver. He climbs up the steps and sits in his seat. Then he vomits. His mother takes him home.

Leslee wakes up complaining of a stomachache. Her mother's rule is if you can't run a fever, throw up, or bleed, you go to school. She is a teacher and doesn't want to stay home with a child who isn't really ill. Leslee comes down to breakfast and eats nothing. Her mother gets her dressed and decides to drive Leslee to school rather than put her on the bus. She wonders if Leslee is stressed about her schoolwork. This is the second time this week that she has complained of a stomachache. As they pull into the school driveway, Leslee starts to breathe rapidly. Her hand starts to shake, and her face changes color.

"What is it, honey?" her mother asks.

Leslee complains about her stomach some more and her mom reassures her that if it continues to bother her throughout the day, she will leave school and come to pick her up. Leslee gets out of the car and wets her pants.

The sympathetic nervous system is engaged when emotions are charged. It is said to *sympathize* with the emotions. This is the alarm stage of the stress syndrome identified by Selye (Sapolsky, 2004). From Chapter 2, we know that normally, information enters the brain through the brain stem and goes to the thalamus, where it is sorted and sent to the neocortex. If the information is worth storing for the long term, the factual part of it goes to the hippocampus, and the emotional part is stored through the amygdala. Both Carl's and Leslee's brains were functioning normally, and they appeared to be calm. But the thought of school made things change. The amygdala and the thalamus reside close to each other. It is said that there is only a single neuron separating them. Because the amygdala of each child was dealing with and remembering the bullying experiences they had, their amygdalae took over their brains and could not look at any-

> The prefrontal cortex usually keeps the amygdala under control, but this is extremely difficult in fearful circumstances.

thing logically. The prefrontal cortex usually keeps the amygdala under control, but this is extremely difficult in fearful circumstances. As a result, their sympathetic nervous systems went into high gear.

When Carl and Leslee anticipated going to school, each amygdala sent an alarm to the hypothalamus. Remember, this is the structure that manages internal messages. First, the hypothalamus sends signals to the adrenal gland to tell it to release epinephrine (also known as adrenaline) and norepinephrine. These two chemicals caused the students' hearts to beat faster and their blood pressure to increase. They also cause faster respiration and stopped digestion. (Since this survival system was set up for predators, the thought has been, why digest when you are worried about being digested yourself?) The blood in their digestive tracts goes to the large muscles in their legs, for flight. At this point, each hypothalamus releases **corticotropin releasing factor (CRF),** which goes to the pituitary gland, located in the brain, conveniently close to the hypothalamus. The pituitary gland then releases **adrenocorticotropic hormone (ACTH),** which stimulates the adrenal glands to produce cortisol. This pathway is commonly called the **HPA (hypothalamus-pituitary-adrenal) axis.**

Cortisol is a stress hormone. It increases the glucose supply to provide more energy for the brain and the heart. It also turns fat into energy and suppresses the reproductive system. As it accomplishes all these tasks, it suppresses the immune system as well (McEwen & Lasley, 2001). All bodily systems sacrifice to prepare the body for what might be its final fight. The importance of immunity, ovulation, and even growth in a child pale in comparison with the task at hand. Yes, had this abuse by their teacher continued very long, their growth could have been stunted. As it was, both children were experiencing extreme responses: Vomiting and loss of bladder control usually occur only in extreme circumstances.

Remember, this *alarm* system was first set up in the days of worrying about attacks by lions and tigers and bears! (Oh, my!) In the case of facing a bully all day, every day, the system becomes even more sensitive.

The children's immune, reproductive, and growth systems were all coming to a screeching halt as the children got closer to that classroom. The amygdalae enjoy the power they have over their brains. However, their hippocampi do not. In fact, the hippocampus can be damaged by too much cortisol and wants to put a stop to its release. While the cortisol circulated in their brains, transmission between neurons may have been interrupted, so the children may not have been be able to think straight. To prevent damage, the hippocampus would send chemical messages to the hypothalamus to stop the release of CRF. But if the amygdala were still sensing danger, it would continue to send signals to the hypothalamus to continue releasing CRF. Once the children were back at home, the hippocampal signals could take charge and stop the stress response (LeDoux, 2002).

This alarm system was first set up in the days of worrying about attacks by lions and tigers and bears! (Oh, my!)

LOOKING FOR BALANCE: THE PARASYMPATHETIC NERVOUS SYSTEM

When the hypothalamus stops releasing CRF, the parasympathetic nervous system takes over. This is the *resistance* phase of the general adaptation syndrome. It tries to create **homeostasis,** or balance, in the body and mind. Saliva production increases, and heart rate decreases. When this system takes over, the students can begin to digest their breakfast (if there is anything left of it!). Their immune and reproductive systems begin their normal work, and their bodies work on repairing any damage done by the stressful situation. This is the *feed and read* response.

This is an important function of the parasympathetic nervous system, and under normal circumstances, it does this well. If stress becomes chronic, however, the hippocampus may become damaged from the cortisol. This damage may cause the hippocampus to weaken and become unable to send a strong message to the hypothalamus to stop releasing CRF. The HPA pathway may then remain activated, and the overload of stress hormones can do further damage to the hippocampus. Along with damage to the hippocampus, there may also be prefrontal lobe damage that can prevent this area of the brain from performing the usual function of controlling the amygdala. Stress-related illnesses might occur because of the suppression of the immune system (McEwen & Lasley, 2001). This describes the *exhaustion* stage of the general adaptation syndrome. The body cannot fight illness, irritability surfaces, and errors are made. The differences between the responses of the parasympathetic and sympathetic nervous systems are summarized in Table 4.1.

Table 4.1 Structures Affected by the Stress Response

Sympathetic Nervous System	Structure	Parasympathetic Nervous System
Dilates pupils	Eyes	Constricts pupils
Inhibits salivation	Mouth	Stimulates salivation
Accelerates heart rate	Heart	Slows heart rate
Bronchial muscles relaxed	Lungs	Bronchial muscles contracted
Inhibits digestion	Intestines	Stimulates digestion
Relaxes urinary bladder	Urinary tract	Stimulates urinary bladder

Possible Results

Carl and Leslee continued to experience stress responses every time they went to school. What is worse, just thinking about Miss Brice started the stress response in their brains, even after she was dismissed from her job. This is an example of the neural or emotional hijacking described in *Emotional Intelligence* (Goleman, 1995). Each amygdala was so sensitive, because of the children's previous experiences, that the amygdala started the stress response before the cerebral cortex had time to process any logical information. The cortisol running through their brains interrupted normal transmission that might have given them the opportunity to take in more information (perhaps it is Saturday and there is no school) and to make a rational decision (e.g., to talk to someone about their teacher, or to remember that she's not there anymore). Their alarm buttons remained on, and their amygdalas continued to anticipate stress.

> "What makes you a coward?" asked Dorothy.
> "It's a mystery," replied the Lion. "I suppose I was born that way."

Allostasis

This term describes a process in which the brain coordinates changes throughout the body, which often leads to changes in behavior (Sapolsky, 2004). Work done by Bruce McEwen (1999) and others has modified the idea of homeostasis to define allostasis: Rather than just balancing the body and trying to get it back to its set point, or ideal state, at the actual time of stress, allostasis assumes that anticipation of stress can also create a need for a response. So, allostasis is the process that deals with change, and *allostatic load* refers to the wear and tear from repeated cycles of allostasis.

You can see how student reactions to stress can change their brains' responses. I once heard the term *phobophobia* and thought it applied so well to many of the situations that we face. Like the Cowardly Lion, many of our students have their alarm buttons turned on. As a result, they are not only afraid, they are also afraid of being afraid. My mother used to tell me that I "borrow trouble." We might say the same things about certain students. They are "borrowing trouble," "hypervigilant," or "afraid of their own shadows." These are all forms of anticipation. These students live in a state of anticipatory stress.

Jenny was one of those students. Any change was almost debilitating for her. In Mrs. Simpson's fifth-grade classroom, Jenny was sometimes beside herself as she anticipated stress.

On one particular Friday, the students were working on some anchor activities for the unit they were studying on mammals. Mrs. Simpson was trying to fix the converter on the TV/VCR, and the noise was interrupting her thinking. She announced that for the following 15 minutes they would have total quiet time. No one could speak.

When Jenny started rocking back and forth vigorously in her desk, Mrs. Simpson noticed out of the corner of her eye and went to the child's desk.

As a result of this anticipatory stress, many students have trouble differentiating between challenge and confrontation, reward and punishment, and surprise and alarm.

"What's the matter, Jenny?" she asked. Jenny was silent. "It's okay, Jenny, you can speak."

"Oh, Mrs. Simpson, I was so worried about not talking. What if there was an emergency? What if I had to go to the bathroom? What if the fire alarm went off? What if . . . ?" The questions were endless. Jenny had anticipated so many possible problems; she had thrown herself into the stress response.

As a result of this anticipatory stress, many students have trouble differentiating between challenge and confrontation, reward and punishment, and surprise and alarm. They do not take in information in the classroom. Some may search the classroom for threats or surprises. Others may daydream as an escape from their feelings (Brownlee, 1996). The appearance and behavior of children under stress can be found on a continuum. Some are mildly stressed, and others are seriously *distressed*. It is this distress that leads to allostatic load.

Look at the possibilities in Table 4.2.

Table 4.2   Levels of Allostatic Load

Stressor	Example	Response
Normal stressor: homework	Homework is finished; stress levels return to normal.	
Chronic stressor: seeing Miss Brice each day	Stress levels go up each time they see or think about her.	
Inability to adapt to novel situations	The new kid at school experiences stress and should eventually feel comfortable; some do not.	
Inability to turn off the stress response	A child who has been treated unfairly or beaten in a competition may be upset and can't let go of it.	
Inability to turn on the stress response	Stress hormones are depleted; the advantages of the stress response are no longer available.	

GIVING THEM COURAGE

During my career, I found three approaches to calm the stress response in my students. The first is predictability, which, as mentioned in Chapter 1, has been defined by experts as one of the basic needs. Creating a safe environment is the second approach. This pertains to emotional as well as physical safety. The final approach involves something I call the *back burner*. This is a way of allowing the students a temporary escape from their feelings and their problems. Let's take each one separately.

Predictability

Isn't it great to know what is going to happen? Jim wakes up in the morning, and Mom has breakfast waiting for him at 7:00 so he can leave the house and catch the bus at the corner at 7:30. He arrives at school at 7:45 with just enough time to get to his locker, put his lunch away, and grab his books for his first-hour class. Mr. Brown is always late for class because he is having his last cup of coffee in the hall while talking to the PE teacher. Mr. Brown enters the room after the bell rings, and Jim knows he can continue talking to his neighbor for another five minutes as Mr. Brown searches for the attendance sheet. This is a predictable situation that allows Jim to feel safe.

Life isn't always like that. I remember walking home from school with my friend, Jamie. She became distressed every day as we approached her street and even somewhat panicky as we came to her house. Many days, she would beg me to come in with her. You see, Jamie's mother was an alcoholic, so Jamie never knew when she walked into the house whether she would be greeted with hugs and kisses or with screams and slaps. Jamie loved school because she felt safe there.

I learned about predictability when I spent a summer vacation traveling and training with Eric Jensen, author of *Teaching With the Brain in Mind* (1998) and many other books. From Eric, I discovered *the use of ritual in the classroom*. I am not talking about hocus-pocus; these rituals are simple repetitive acts that become predictable. It is a stimulus-response situation. Whenever a particular situation occurs, a particular response will follow.

You can compare a ritual with a tradition. It is traditional on Christmas Eve for my family to be with my husband's family to exchange presents. Stimulus: Christmas Eve. Response: present exchange with the Sprengers. It is a tradition at our house to go out to dinner at a specific restaurant the night before the first day of the school year. Stimulus: eve of the first day of school. Response: dinner at Lum's. The family counts on these traditions. If they do not occur, it just doesn't *feel* right. It is very uncomfortable. Traditions are difficult to break because of the feeling of security that comes with their predictability.

 You can compare a ritual with a tradition.

Classrooms need many rituals to provide this feeling of security, which may help de-stress the students. I tell my workshop participants that they need to have 15 to 20 rituals in place by the end of the first week of school. If that number seems high, you may change your mind as I give you some examples. This is not a magic formula. You must decide what will work in your classroom with your children.

This is what happens at the beginning of my class: As the students enter, "Be True to Your School," by the Beach Boys, is playing. I am standing at the door, greeting my students with a smile and a "Good morning!" When the tardy bell rings, I walk to the CD player and turn off the music. I turn to the students who are sitting with their teammates and say, "If you have 100 percent of your teammates seated and ready to go, raise your hand, and say 'Yes!'" The students raise their hands, and when I see which teams do not have their hands up, I check to see who is absent. This is a quick and easy way to take attendance. Then, I say, "Turn to the person next to you and say, 'Good morning, I'm happy you're here today!'" My next step is to go to the lunch menu. I become the world's worst salesperson as I "sell" lunch. "Who wants green hot dogs today? We have greasy fries and a soggy cookie to dress up that ugly cafeteria tray! What do you say—raise your hand if you want lunch!" (Fortunately for me, the cafeteria staff never found out about this!)

In that five-minute homeroom period, I had five rituals: (1) the music, (2) greeting at the door, (3) taking attendance, (4) saying something to a teammate, and (5) selling lunch. To assign rituals to situations, you must first think of the situations you might encounter in your particular classroom. Remember that these do not have to occur on a daily basis. These are rituals that fit situations. As long as you perform the ritual whenever the situation occurs, you are using this technique properly.

- What will you do for someone's birthday? (I always play a silly tape of cats meowing the happy birthday song.)
- What will you do for the opening of class? (I play that song by the Beach Boys.)
- What will you do for the closing of class? (How about playing "Happy Trails to You"?)
- What will you do when a student is going to read his or her written work aloud? (I have an "author's hat" the student must wear.)
- What will you do when a visitor interrupts the class? (I teach my students to stand up and applaud! We don't often get visitors anymore unless they are hams!)
- What will you do when it is lunchtime? (I say, "Turn to the person next to you and say, 'I'm hungry!'")
- What will you do on a test day? (I play "Celebration" because we are celebrating our learning.)
- What will you do to dismiss the class? (Turn to the person next to you and say, "'I grew dendrites today!'" Then, stand at the door and give each student a "high five" as he or she exits.)
- What will you do on library day? Music day? Art day? Computer day?

Think about rituals that will work for you and your students. You must be comfortable with your ritual so your students will be, too. Some examples can be found in Table 4.3.

Table 4.3   Suggestions for Classroom Rituals

Situation	Ritual
Opening of class	• Familiar music being played • Students meet in small groups to check homework • Daily oral language, math, geography, etc. • Journal activities • Shaking hands of all students as they enter • Short problem on overhead projector • Movement activities • A clapping ritual to get their attention
Ending of class	• Familiar music being played • Exit cards required • Quick recap of important points • Students repeat aloud what their homework assignment is
Birthdays	• Favorite birthday song: Beatles, traditional, etc. • Sheet of paper is sent around room for positive comments • Treats are provided by teacher • Birthday person has special seat, hat, etc.
Test days	• Students may play quiet games after test • Special test music is played • Special movement activities (e.g., brain gym as explained in Chapter 5)
Special presentations (oral reports, etc.)	• Music (from *Chariots of Fire, Rocky,* etc.) • Presentation hat or chair
Going to special classes (computer, art, music)	• Play a get-ready song like "Hi Ho"
Attendance	• Answering with a new vocabulary word • Or a word from the Word Wall
Review	• Each one, teach one: Students pair up and review • Mind-map the material • *Jeopardy* or trivia game

Will your class become boring? Predictability puts students at ease so you can use novelty. If every day you do exactly the same thing in a very repetitive manner, both you and your students may get bored. And boredom can be stressful! Balance is important. Rituals make room for challenge, novelty, and a little craziness, which make the classroom fun. Can you change your ritual? Absolutely. Just keep in mind that it will take some time for your students to become accustomed to the new one, and be sure to warn them before you change. Be predictable!

So far, I have covered 18 possible rituals or situations for rituals. Get your principal involved. Ask him or her to use a specific phrase when ending announcements. Mine always says, "And have a great day!" When our principal is absent and someone else gives the announcements, the students are very disappointed if they don't start their day with that phrase. I have even had kids at the end of the day tell me that they had a rotten day and it was all because our principal wasn't there to tell them to have a great day. Predictability is that important.

In Addition to Rituals, Classroom Rules Are Very Important

Classroom rules provide security as long as you stick to them. Be sure that students understand the rules. It is always good to have the students help you make them. Post them, send them home, and follow them. They become like rituals if you consistently use the same consequences for breaking them.

Give Overviews

Students need to know what they are going to be doing each day. Create a mind map (a diagram with words or pictures centered around a single topic or idea) or outline on the board each day with the schedule of events. This will help your students de-stress. Knowing what is going to happen, even if it is painful, gives students a feeling like, "Okay, I know we are going to do long division today, but I can get through it." (It's like going to the dentist. If I know he has another appointment 30 minutes after mine, I can cope, knowing it won't last too long.)

Make Homework Assignments Visible

Choose a spot to display the day's homework. I know sometimes it is difficult to know how far you will get with a lesson, so it may not be possible to put the assignment up before class begins. Stop your lesson a few minutes early and give students time to copy the assignment as you display it.

Provide Students With Good Work Samples, So They Know Your Expectations

Whether you expect good essays, formal projects, or informal papers, students need to see clearly what your expectations are. Samples from previous years or examples that you and the class create together can lower stress levels greatly (Stiggins et al., 2005). How will they know what you want unless you show them? This will not take away their creativity. It will lower their stress levels and allow them to be more creative in their work. If you have a rubric that you are using to assess their work, provide the rubric as well.

Safe Environment

Creating an environment in which students feel physically safe is difficult after the recent shooting incidents at schools. After the Columbine High School shootings in Littleton, Colorado, I spent part of my teaching time for several days discussing safety and escape possibilities with my students. It began with many of them gathering around me in the library, getting as physically close to me as seventh graders will allow themselves to, and asking me what I would do if the situation should arise. We spoke of fear and the fight-or-flight response. We discussed alternate routes from the library and from our classroom. I emphasized the relative safety of our building, our PA system, and the current awareness generated by the recent incidents. They needed to talk about these issues, and by doing so, they felt safer.

We may not be able to guarantee their safety, but we can assure them of our concern for it.

For students to feel physical safety, they must first have emotional safety with us as their teachers—their guardians for the time they are with us. This is accomplished both verbally and nonverbally. Students must know that we walk the talk. Our words, our actions, our facial expressions, and our body language must all be congruent. A message is only 7 percent content; it is 38 percent voice (tonality, tempo, volume, and timbre) and 55 percent body language (gestures, position, and proximity). For this reason, teachers must say what they mean and mean what they say. Sarcasm cannot enter the classroom. Neither the teacher nor the students must be allowed to tease or joke in any manner that might hurt someone. Your students must know that they will be supported as unconditionally as possible.

Inappropriate discipline or embarrassing situations cause biological and chemical reactions. Yes, mere spoken words that are critical or sarcastic, when heard on a daily basis, can change the brain. The words are converted to nerve signals that move along the auditory nerves to reach the temporal lobes. These signals are dispersed throughout the brain, and they activate specific networks of neurons. At this neuronal level, changes are made that eventually lead to changes in the nucleus of the cell, which can actually cause genes to be repressed or activated. Some of our genes would never be activated if certain conditions were not present. So if a child has a gene that gives him or her a tendency toward depression, repeated experiences of sarcastic or cutting remarks could cause it to be expressed (Restak, 2000). Conversely, if the child experiences consistently kind and respectful treatment, the gene may never be expressed,

> For students to feel physical safety, they must first have emotional safety with us as their teachers—their guardians for the time they are with us.

and the child may never develop symptoms of depression. Interactions in the classroom must be nonthreatening, so the brain can be relaxed enough to look for patterns and make connections.

Safety Can Be Felt in Surroundings

Is your classroom pleasant to walk into? Although many classrooms have limited natural light, make use of what you have. Sunshine causes the release of neurotransmitters that make us feel good. Are there pictures, posters, stuffed animals, or memorabilia in your room? In 1973, I purchased a poster of a wall of graffiti. It had quotations on it, such as "I think; therefore, I am." My students love this poster. All the material on it is positive, and they think it relates to them. How about making your own with quotations from your students? I also keep stuffed animals around the room. Even high school students will occasionally grab one when they need some closeness. It makes the room look inviting—a little like home. (Once, a colleague entered my seventh-grade room and said, "This looks like a bedroom!" I took that as a compliment.) Students of all ages relate to music of some kind. If you are not comfortable playing it, at least have a CD player in your classroom available for soothing music.

Accessibility to Water and Bathrooms Creates a Safer Place for Students

This may not seem important, but to many students it is. There are some classrooms in which using bathrooms or getting drinks is not allowed or is allowed only at certain designated times. Keep in mind that students are not able to learn if these needs are not met. If this privilege becomes abused, issue students a designated number of bathroom passes each grading period. Unused passes may be redeemed for something special. I have even given minimal extra-credit points for unused passes. (The thought behind this is that the student was in the classroom more and probably absorbed more learning!) Humans need to drink at least eight glasses of water per day. The brain is made up of 80 percent water. Dehydrating the brain causes poor learning (Jensen, 2005).

Back Burner

I stole this idea from a teacher in one of my workshops many years ago. I do not remember her name, but I want to thank her. I have used this concept ever since and believe it adds to the safety and security of my classroom.

Students often enter our classrooms with their alarm buttons on. It is our first priority to teach all our students. If the stress response is in motion, they will not have the opportunity to learn. To give them an opportunity to put their thoughts and problems on the back burner, we do the following: Any day that I feel it is necessary, or if a student requests, students take a few minutes at the beginning of class and write down anything that is bothering them. The slip of paper is folded and stored in a box on my desk. In this symbolic way, their problems are no longer with them. When I first introduce the strategy, I tell them how sometimes, we have important things to attend to. Our attention is difficult to divide. If we put our problems on hold while we do our work, I make sure that later in the day, we have time to go back and look at what the students have written. If the problem is still important, they may take the time to discuss it with someone in the classroom. What is interesting is that most of those problems are no longer problems later in the day. Many of them are small disagreements or concerns about virtually unimportant items. After giving the students time away from these interferences, they often realize that what they thought was a big deal no longer is one.

If the stress response is in motion, they will not have the opportunity to learn.

Giving students the opportunity to put their issues aside gives me the chance to halt the stress response and begin the learning response.

I have had several students request the back burner activity. Usually the circumstances were school related. With short classes at the middle and high school levels, I found that turning over the responsibility of calling for the process to the students worked quite well. They could let me know with a gesture, verbally, or in writing. Sometimes the written request would get to me after I had started a lesson. This interruption was sometimes frustrating, but I tried not to let them know this.

At times like this, a change in plan is necessary. With tension in the room, I knew I would get nowhere with the lesson I had planned. Because of the safe environment I had created and the rituals that were in place, I was able to give the students the chance to work things out without the threat of losing total control of the class. There will be times when alarm buttons are on and nothing I do will switch them off. At least with these strategies, I have a chance to tame those lions.

We're Off to See . . .

Stress and emotion are closely related, and some researchers consider stress one of our emotions. In the next chapter, we will look at emotions and emotional intelligences. Strategies will be offered to improve our students' abilities to handle stress and other emotions so they can improve learning.

WIZDOM

Key Points to Ponder

1. Understanding stress will help us deal with the stress of our students.

2. Providing rituals in the classroom offers the brain predictability, which it needs in order to avoid initiating the stress response.

3. Acknowledging your students' need to release stress will strengthen the relationships you have with them.

Suggestions

- Realize that you may stress some students. Try to identify those students and discover a way to lower their stress.
- Just as mimicking is the way students learn empathy, it is also the way they learn to be sarcastic or to tease. Teach your students to be good role models for others.
- Keep in mind that ritual is more than a routine. Taking attendance every day by calling students' names and waiting for a reply is boring and time-consuming. Unless you are making a connection through this procedure that engages the class, you are probably offering students time to become bored and misbehave. Make your ritual relevant and timely.
- Use the checklist in Figure 4.1 to determine if you are keeping stress levels low.

Figure 4.1   Checklist for Lowering Stress

Checklist for Lowering Stress

_____   1. I am providing a warm environment.

_____   2. We have made our classroom rules and are following them.

_____   3. I provide a daily preview or overview of what we will be doing.

_____   4. My students have access to water when needed.

_____   5. My students have bathroom privileges when needed.

_____   6. Homework assignments are visually displayed.

_____   7. Students know what I want them to learn from the topic.

_____   8. Work samples are available to students, so they can see good examples.

_____   9. Student work is displayed in the room.

_____   10. I have eliminated sarcasm from my classroom.

---

5 If I Only Had a Heart

Emotional Growth

You people with hearts have something to guide you and need never do wrong; but I have no heart, and so I must be very careful.

—The Tin Woodsman

"That's mine. Put it down!" Janelle screamed from the back of the room.

"I just want to see it for a minute!" Andrea yelled back. "You're such a creep. I can't believe how selfish you are." She trudges back to her seat.

"What's the problem here?" I ask Janelle.

"I just bought this new purse," Janelle states emphatically. "And I don't want her touching it. She'll just get it dirty."

I look at the designer purse. I assume that it's a fake. I can't imagine Janelle's family paying a thousand dollars for an original. But I could be wrong. The purse is made of a material I call "vinyl-coated plastic." Many good purses are made of this material as it is easy to keep clean and doesn't scratch like leather.

"She's a thief," Janelle continues. "She took Kindra's money out of her locker a few weeks ago."

Suddenly this conversation is getting dangerous. I don't want the other students to overhear these comments. True or not, it hurts the social and emotional environment of the classroom.

"Janelle, let's talk outside for a few minutes," I suggest. "Andrea, why don't you join us?"

We head to the hallway. My students settle back to their work. I hear rumblings from Andrea and Janelle's team as I leave. I stop and say, "I'd appreciate if you would keep your conversation on the assignment." The students quiet down and get back on task.

When the three of us are in the hall, I ask for an account of what occurred first from Andrea and then from Janelle.

"I asked her if I could see her crummy purse, and she said no. I just wanted to see what it felt like . . . and I did not steal any money!"

"Yeah, I said no. That you could see it later at lunch. But you went and grabbed it anyway!" Janelle screamed again.

"Hold it down, please," I say to Janelle. "Andrea, you owe Janelle an apology if she asked you to wait. Sometimes we just have to control our impulses. It's a very pretty purse." (I smile at Janelle.) "But you two were working on an assignment and you have to wait for this kind of socializing until we are finished."

"I'll apologize if Janelle takes back what she said about me stealing Kindra's money. Just ask Kindra; she found her money in the bottom of that junk in her locker."

Janelle looks a bit sheepish. "Okay, I shouldn't have said that. But you made me so mad!!"

We go back into the room and the girls get back to work. They seem to be fine. I, on the other hand, am exhausted.

Emotional coaching is time-consuming and energy zapping. But it's part of what teaching is about these days. Unfortunately, not all parents are good emotional coaches, and that leaves yet another thing to teachers. Daniel Goleman's groundbreaking book, *Emotional Intelligence*, opened many of our eyes to what students lack. In 1995, when the book was published, he focused on five areas or elements of emotional intelligence:

1. Self-awareness
2. Managing emotions
3. Self-motivation
4. Recognizing the emotions of others
5. Handling relationships

Although these may seem like very tall orders for many of our students, we hope—and it is likely—that most of them will enter school with these skills. Goleman has since written several more books on the subject and has made the list a little more manageable with four components: self-awareness, self-management, social awareness, and relationship management (Goleman et al., 2002). I like working with the four elements (shown in Table 5.1), although they still cover all five of the original components.

The progression is simple. We must recognize our own emotions before we know how to control them. Once they are controlled—and this includes

Table 5.1   Elements of Emotional Intelligence

Elements of Emotional Intelligence	Description
Self-Awareness	The ability to recognize one's own emotions in various situations. This is a result of others recognizing those emotions in you and helping you label them.
Self-Management	The ability to take those emotions and handle them in different situations. Coaching by caregivers is the strongest way this skill is developed.
Social Awareness	Recognizing the emotions of others. When one can recognize his or her own emotions and control them, then one can sense how others are feeling and empathize with them.
Relationship Management	Upon recognizing how others are feeling, one can take those feelings into consideration when dealing with relationships with individuals.

SOURCE: Adapted from Goleman et al. (2002).

impulsivity—which Andrea was having trouble with—then we are able to recognize the emotions of others. If Andrea had been able to control her impulsivity, then perhaps she would have been able to see that Janelle was really feeling possessive about her new purse, and Andrea would have left her alone about it. In recognizing how others are feeling, Andrea can better handle the relationship she has with Janelle. In Janelle's case, she

> The progression is simple. We must recognize our own emotions before we know how to control them.

obviously wasn't doing a very good job of managing her own emotions as was evidenced by her lashing out at Andrea about stealing. Perhaps Janelle wasn't recognizing her own problem with sharing.

What may happen at home to develop these elements is worth looking at because we are often expected to duplicate conditions that encourage the practice of these skills. The period from cradle to school ranges from two to five years for our students. Yet the opportunity to develop emotional intelligence begins in the cradle.

HEARTBREAK: THE LACK OF SOCIAL AND EMOTIONAL STIMULATION

We know from the horrifying Romanian orphan situations that social and emotional growth is not possible without human contact. The positron emission tomography (PET) scans of those orphans showed huge vacant areas in their brains when compared with those of children who had been raised with affection, conversation, and love (McCormick Tribune Foundation, 2004). The theory behind raising the orphans in Romania without attachments made sense to the caregivers. Because the turnover in help was so high, they were afraid that the children would become attached to someone only to lose him or her shortly thereafter. The trauma of constant separations appeared to be more harmful than the emotional neglect the children experienced (McCormick Tribune Foundation, 2004). The behavior of the children varied from continual rocking and mumbling to some aggression. With love and attention, many of these children are now leading normal lives (Fischer, 1999). A small percentage still has emotional and behavioral problems, and these children may have them the rest of their lives.

Experiments done in the 1950s with monkeys revealed the same types of reactions. Baby monkeys who had been isolated for several months and were then placed back into "society" exhibited strange behaviors. The monkeys showed cognitive deficits as well as immune deficiencies. The immune problems may well have been from the stress these monkeys experienced through their isolation. The serotonin levels of these babies were abnormal; for some, this caused aggressiveness and for others, acquiescence. They also had trouble mating, and many abused their own babies (Barnet & Barnet, 1998). These are extreme cases. All mammals have a basic need for mothering, and they all fear abandonment. Indeed, a separation period of a mere 24 hours can cause physical changes in an infant's blood pressure, responsiveness, and heart rate (Ramey & Ramey, 1999).

Many kinds of violence can cause harm to a child's brain and affect emotional and social abilities. A single incident has the power to alter the brain's chemistry and arouse fear and suspicion that could lead to depression or drug abuse. Because of the brain's plasticity, much can be overcome. In cases of consistent abuse and neglect, children are constantly hypervigilant, looking for danger in every face and around every corner. They may be scanning their teachers' faces for threat or punishment, with hearts racing and cortisol levels high. An innocent nudge or bump on the playground may be misinterpreted and lead to inappropriate reactions (Brownlee, 1996).

> Many kinds of violence can cause harm to a child's brain and affect emotional and social abilities.

CREATING HEART:
A LOOK AT EMOTIONAL INTELLIGENCE

What should normally occur to provide children with normal brain chemistries and appropriate social development? At this point, we are going to look at a healthy child, let's say a little girl, in a healthy environment. We will assume that nothing interfered with the migration of neurons and that the child was born with normal birth weight and has a caretaker with whom to bond.

The first important point is that the child has someone to respond to her needs. At this very early stage, the infant learns that her needs are important. Thus she becomes aware of her self. She becomes hungry and cries, and her mother comes to feed her. This affirmation is the beginning of an understanding of her value. Along with this knowledge comes the assumption that the world is a very safe place. In other words, the baby can predict on a regular basis what is going to happen in her world. She understands that her feelings are important and will be addressed.

The atmosphere of this early care appears to affect the brain structure, the amygdala. This area of the brain is related to emotions. We saw how sensitive this structure can be to stress, and the early phases of a child's life can have a great effect in this way. The amygdala receives highly sensitive information from many brain areas. In turn, it calls on the structures that affect bodily functions, such as heart rate (Brothers, 1997). It is very important that the early sensory information be soothing and reassuring.

Babies can also learn to manage their emotions in the crib. Initially, whenever the infant is upset, a caregiver promptly arrives and calms the child. When her world is safe and secure, she eventually begins to calm herself. This is the first opportunity for her to manage her emotions. As the child leaves the crib and continues a safe relationship with the primary people in her life, her self-awareness and handling of emotions continue; however, the adults in her life must model the appropriate behavior. In other words, her role models also act as emotional coaches and help the infant and young child work through her emotions.

The result of responsive, supportive feedback offers the child a confident outlook and encourages exploration and learning (Ramey & Ramey, 1999). In this way, the self-motivation area of emotional intelligence naturally emerges. As understanding responses are received, the child ventures out to discover more of the world. The knowledge that someone is nearby and will react to her needs allows greater motivation to explore and conquer new areas.

We must look at impulse control in the area of self-motivation. This skill is imperative in the successful child. If one can control one's impulses, one is less likely to behave in a manner that concludes with inappropriate results. Impulse control can be learned. Goleman (1995) refers to the "marshmallow experiments" of the 1960s, in which researchers at Stanford University did a study of four-year-old preschoolers. These children were each offered a marshmallow and told that the experimenter had to leave the room. If they waited to eat the marshmallow until the experimenter returned, they would receive two marshmallows. Waiting was an impossible task for some of the children, but some did wait a seemingly very long time and managed to get the second treat.

 We must look at impulse control in the area of self-motivation.

What was amazing about this simple test was its later consequences. As these children were tracked up to 14 years later, it was discovered that those who had resisted impulse and delayed gratification handled life more easily. They appeared to be less stressed, dealt with pressure more easily than those in the group that could not wait for the experimenter, and had higher scores on their scholastic achievement tests (SATs). Good impulse control at an early age is a strong predictor of later success. What is especially comforting to us as teachers is that delay of gratification and impulse control can be learned. Students may come to school possessing these skills, because their parents simply insisted that all their vegetables be eaten before dessert or that their rooms be cleaned before they watched television.

Recognizing the emotions of others is an empathic act that actually begins before the infant realizes that there are others. Studies have shown that babies in cribs will cry when they see or hear the cries of others. At two or three years of age, toddlers are still not sure that the pain or discomfort of others is not their own. Even at the toddling age, one may see empathy in the young child who tries to comfort another who is crying. Some will offer the upset child a blanket or toy. The comfort that he or she received enables the individual to offer empathy to others. Children who have not been responded to and acknowledged in a positive fashion may approach other crying children and yell at them to stop or perhaps slap them. This is indicative of the kind of responsiveness children have received.

According to Hoffman (Barnet & Barnet, 1998), there are four stages in the development of empathy. In Stage 1, the infant becomes distressed at the cries of another. Stage 2 is egocentric. At this point, children imitate the distress of others. In Stage 3, which seems to occur around the ages of two or three, children know that the distress is not their own, and they try to comfort others. During the school years, at around age eight, the final stage of empathy develops. This stage is more global in form. The child can use his or her imagination to help understand the pleasure or pain another is feeling. Different experiences have helped shaped the child's responses to the emotions of others, and he or she can begin to feel empathic toward large groups of people, such as those surviving disasters or disease.

The ability of children to be empathic comes from mimicking what they have seen modeled by the adults around them. When a caregiver recognizes a child's emotion and responds in a way that lets the child know the emotion is understood, empathy is being modeled and may develop. This type of interaction may include signals, eye contact, or dialogue. Empathic behavior is an important component of emotional and social intelligence that is lacking in many career criminals. They have no idea how someone else might feel. Therefore, hurting others does not seem to make them remorseful in any way (Goleman, 1995).

> **The ability of children to be empathic comes from mimicking what they have seen modeled by the adults around them.**

Again, the brain structure that appears to deal with empathy is the amygdala. This area responds to different facial expressions. The more activity found in the amygdala when subjects are shown specific expressions, the more socially sensitive the subjects seem to be. Damage in this area, in parts of the temporal lobe, or in the frontal lobe may cause an individual to be incapable of judging the feelings of others and result in an inability to make social connections.

Handling relationships is an emotional and social skill that can easily result from acquiring the preceding intelligence skills. If an individual is aware of his or her emotions, manages them, is self-motivated, and can show empathy for others, it makes sense that the individual will get along with other people. However, this is a learned skill that can easily be overlooked in the preschool years. This skill falls under Howard Gardner's definition of interpersonal intelligence. It includes the ability to organize groups and influence them as well as to analyze situations and gain rapport with individuals in various situations (Gardner, 1985).

The interaction between child and caretaker is the beginning of this skill. It may be reinforced and enhanced through play groups, family interactions, and preschool. Through practice, play, and mimicking adult behavior, children learn to persuade, influence, inspire, and create intimate relationships—skills that can take them far in life.

HEART-TO-HEART

Benny and Aaron have been friends for as long as either of them can remember. They grew up in the same neighborhood, their mothers shopped at the same corner grocery, and they know all the kids on the block. Today, they are walking to school together the way they have since kindergarten. They talk about their favorite teachers and fool around until they are on the playground with the other children. Benny wants to swing, and Aaron follows slowly over to the swing set, where several children are playing.

Benny yells, "Hey, you guys, it's our turn now. Somebody get off." Most of the children are too busy to pay any attention to Benny, and those that notice him continue to swing.

"I said you should get off the swing now. You've had it long enough. I want to swing." There is still no response. Benny walks over to a small boy on the swing and grabs the rope. This action causes a jerky movement and the swing stops suddenly. The boy almost falls off but manages to keep his balance. The child begins to cry as Benny continues ranting about his turn.

By this time, Aaron has arrived at the messy scene. He knows the small boy on the swing, whose name is Will. "Whatsa matter, Willy?" asks Aaron.

Benny blurts out, "He won't get off the swing, and it's my turn!"

Aaron puts his arm around Willy and looks at Benny. "We just got here, Benny. We haven't waited for our turn yet. Let's go down the slide while Willy finishes swinging. Then maybe we can have his swing."

Willy nods his head and wipes his tears with his sleeve. Aaron takes Benny's arm and guides him toward the slide. Benny turns around, glares at Willy, and shouts, "You better be done soon, that's all I can say!"

Two boys from the same neighborhood are trying to get along in this world of the school. One chooses tact and negotiation because he has seen effective outcomes using these; the other chooses to be pushy and powerful as that is what has been modeled for him. We know who will be more successful if from this point there is no further emotional and social growth. Can school effect these positive changes?

STRAIGHT FROM THE HEART: SOCIAL AND EMOTIONAL INTELLIGENCE STRATEGIES

 Emotional intelligence can be taught.

As the Tin Man went on Dorothy's journey, he was provided with opportunities to use the heart he thought was missing. Situations allowed him to use the emotional intelligence he already had and to develop it more while he was on the road. Children need those same opportunities. Emotional intelligence (sometimes referred to as EQ, as it is compared to the intelligence quotient, IQ) can be taught, and I found that incorporating it into the classroom was natural for me and for my students.

There are eight things I keep in mind as I set up my classroom and the atmosphere in it. These strategies fit in with the emotional intelligence categories quite nicely. As you look at Table 5.2, you can see how I utilize these activities and games to promote the specific EQ components. You may think of many others that would be useful to you and your classroom.

- Pretend play/role-play
- Mind reading
- Teaming/grouping
- Delaying gratification
- Choices
- Rapport skills
- Journaling
- Physical outlets

Pretend Play/Role-Play

Because the brain is so underdeveloped at birth, we as a society must commit ourselves to the 20 or so years it takes for full brain development in our children. For our children to become acting members of the civilization in which they live, they need practice. If that sounds funny, think about what childhood and adolescence really are—a time to figure out where to fit in and how.

Every society has rules and regulations, and children must learn them. This is a gradual process acquired through their environments. To practice these rules, children use play (Brothers, 1997). In their play, they become others, often adults, who are either following the established rules or disobeying them. In other words, they are trying on different roles and finding which ones suit them.

Pretending is encouraged in many environments while children are very young, but in school, little time is made for this activity. The costume and dress-up corners often seen at preschools and in some kindergartens are usually gone by the primary grades. These opportunities are very important in the context of social and emotional growth. Children take the mental scripts—from their personal experiences or those they have viewed on television or read in books—and share them with other children. As the children share these social scenes, interaction takes place in which each child involved has the opportunity to change. They may agree with the interactions of others, disagree and explain, or possibly ask an adult or other child to settle a dispute about the way things are supposed to happen. Social rules are learned and reinforced.

Table 5.2   Social-Emotional Skills for Different Grade Levels and
Strategies for Learning Them

Grade Level	Self-Awareness	Self-Management	Social Awareness	Relationship Management
Early Elementary	Recognize and label emotions.	Demonstrate control of impulsive behavior.	Recognize that others experience situations differently from oneself.	Identify ways to play and work well with others.
Late Elementary	Describe a range of emotions and their causes.	Describe and demonstrate how emotions should be displayed.	Identify verbal, physical, and situational cues that indicate how others feel.	Describe ways to make and keep friends.
Middle/Junior High	Analyze factors that create emotion.	Apply strategies to self-motivate.	Predict others' feelings in a variety of situations.	Analyze ways to create positive relationships with others.
Early High School	Analyze how emotions affect behavior.	Create ways to develop positive attitudes.	Analyze similarities and differences between one's own and others' perspectives.	Evaluate the effects of asking for support from others and providing it.
Late High School	Evaluate how emotions affect others.	Evaluate the influence of positive attitudes.	Demonstrate how to express understanding of those who hold different opinions.	Evaluate the application of communication skills and social skills when interacting with others, including teachers, peers, and family.
Strategies for Learning	Mind reading Journaling	Mind reading Delaying gratification Journaling Role-playing Making choices	Teaming Rapport building Role-playing Making choices	Teaming Rapport building Role-playing Making choices

In the eyes of older children, the idea of pretending is too immature. This is where role-play allows for the same social rules to emerge. Regardless of what the content of the class might be, there are opportunities to use role-play as a valid activity to reinforce learning. In social studies, groups could role-play a scene taking place in a Southern home during the Civil War. Discussion of feelings and events may follow. A reenactment of the Boston Tea Party has been done successfully, with observable changes in attitude and behavior by the actors after having put themselves in someone else's shoes. Literature is easily conducive to this activity, as is a writing class. Math calls for role-play in making change, taking measurements, and discussing geometric figures and algebraic equations. Clever science teachers have even used role-play in the form of students becoming elements of the periodic table and discussing the possible outcomes of "becoming involved with each other."

We have little time for play in school because of the pressures of preparing students for standardized testing and our need to cover the curriculum. However, we must remember those marshmallow kids who scored higher on their SATs, seemingly because their emotional intelligence was high.

Mind Reading

This is a game I made up. It needn't be called "Mind Reading", but it actually is fun and beneficial for many of our students. Many studies have suggested that some people have difficulty reading faces. That is, they are not able to accurately relate the expression on another's face to the actual emotion being experienced by the person. Many scientists believe that facial expressions are actions of inner feelings. They are a form of social communication (Brothers, 1997). Therefore, it becomes important that children be able to read faces and respond appropriately.

We know from current research that emotions drive attention and attention drives learning (Sylwester, 2000). Students who don't read expressions well may get messages confused. This can cause emotional turmoil that will keep their attention away from the task at hand. We must do what we can to help students separate emotions. A study was done of girls in the seventh through tenth grades. Results indicated that eating disorders among these girls were affected by the fact that they had difficulty differentiating one feeling from another (Goleman, 1995). Some people cannot tell the difference between feeling angry, hungry, and afraid. They combine these feelings into one and try to eat their way out of the emotion. I found that using some funny faces made it easier for my students to sort out their own feelings.

From culture to culture, people seem to recognize and read six basic expressions: fear, anger, sadness, disgust, happiness, and surprise. The ability to read these expressions may be based on survival. As a species or as a culture, it may have been imperative that we were able to assess strangers as enemies or friends simply by reading their facial expressions. Because our emotional system has direct wiring to our facial muscles, looking into someone's eyes and checking their mouths for a smile or a frown may give us enough information to know whether to approach or avoid a person (Johnson, 2004). Unfortunately, not all children are able to read faces. In my years of training teachers in brain-compatible strategies, I have been amazed at how many teachers have shown concern for the number of children misreading social cues, including facial expression. Some studies done at the University of Wisconsin have shown that abused children not only overreact to pictures of angry faces but also misread other expressions as anger (Blum, 1998). These children may need to be ready for anger at home, but becoming defensive or fearful at school when misreading the expressions of others may lead to real trouble.

 From culture to culture, people seem to recognize and read six basic expressions: fear, anger, sadness, disgust, happiness, and surprise.

So, mind reading became my game. It begins with a poster showing different facial expressions. I hang it on my door so the students see it as they enter and exit. After a few weeks, I ask the classes if anyone has noticed the poster. I have heard several comments about the poster by then, so I know I will get some acknowledgment. We start discussing the various expressions and what they mean. This is something I do when I have a few minutes to spare.

Then, I draw some pictures of my own (see Figure 5.1). My artwork leaves a lot to be desired, but, amazingly, I get the desired point across. I put four faces on an overhead or make handouts. They do not have the expression in writing beneath each face as the poster does. I have the students do some mind reading as to what the person is feeling. The six basic expressions are the ones I start with and mix up. Then, I begin adding some of the other expressions from the poster. These are a little more difficult to discern, but the kids have a great time trying to figure them out. Along with the recognition of the expression, we add stories explaining why the person feels that way. We practice making the same faces ourselves. This adds to the fun and gives the students the opportunity to see how the expressions of some people are a little different from those of others.

Next, I begin to hold up a face every day as they come in. I put an expressive look on my face and hold up the face that shows how I feel. The kids tell me how I feel and try to guess why. Eventually, everyone gets a stack of faces and as soon as everyone is seated, they each hold up a face. I have the option of asking them why they feel that way or letting them find a partner to do that. We become

Figure 5.1 Drawings Used in the Mind Reading Game

NOTE: Students have to guess what the facial expression represents.

quite good at it, and the students become more emotionally involved with me and with each other, which leads to a more secure classroom.

Through this activity my students are able to become aware of their emotions, read the emotions of others, in some cases express empathy, and manage their own emotions. For the little time it takes, the activity helps them develop many of the emotional intelligences and is well worth it.

The value of reading the expressions of others can be shared at any grade level. In the upper grades, this type of activity may be taught as a skill that would be helpful in the job market. Getting and keeping one's job could be dependent on understanding how others are feeling and knowing how to deal with it (Goleman et al., 2002). Using this type of strategy in a career class or unit may make the class more realistic and enable students to relate what they are learning to previous experiences. Mind reading could also be integrated into social studies, science, or reading. (How was the character feeling? What did he look like when he felt that way?)

> **The value of reading the expressions of others can be shared at any grade level.**

There are other great ideas for developing self-awareness that you may find more interesting. Goleman (1995) mentions a strategy that deals with attendance. As the student's name is called, the student says "Here" and adds a number from one to ten. The number one means that the student is happy, and ten indicates that the student is not having a great day. The numbers in between indicate varying levels of happiness. The students may give reasons for the number if they choose. There are variations of this strategy, which have worked very well when I have used it.

Another clever idea is to read Dr. Seuss's *My Many Colored Days* (Seuss, Johnson, & Fancher, 1998) to the students. Let me assure you that students of every age can appreciate this book. There is also a video available of the book, which may be a preferable option for you. After understanding what feeling each color represents, you can have colored strips of paper or cards at the door as the students enter. Each student picks a card to indicate how he or she is feeling. This may be used as a cue for you, or it may be used as the basis for a discussion. Whatever strategy you choose, you will be honoring each student's feelings, which will further your personal relationships with your students.

Teaming/Grouping

Just as Dorothy needed her team of the Cowardly Lion, the Scarecrow, and the Tin Man, your students also need a feeling of belonging. I cannot say enough about the importance of this strategy. I began using it in 1992 on a regular basis. Teaming can solve a number of problems. Putting your students on teams can make teaching and learning more fun. It makes taking attendance easier. It enables students to give each other positive feedback that may increase their serotonin levels, which may make them calmer and happier. It gives students a feeling of belonging, which is one of the basic needs. It enables students to learn and practice the emotional and social skills that are necessary for success in school and in life.

Teams don't just happen. Students need to know what the expectations of the team are. Discussing possible team problems and role-playing some of those may be necessary if your students have not experienced this type of learning situation. There are steps in team-building to aid the feeling of belonging. As a primary human motivation, belonging is essential. Humans try to belong by imitation, contagion, or identification (Brothers, 1997). Contagion can be positive, as in being part of a cheering crowd at a football game, but, in general, it is less productive than the other two forms. Imitation is how children first learn. Mothers tend to imitate babies, who then imitate back. As babies and small children begin to imitate adults, it is gratifying and affords some special bonding (Gopnik, Meltzoff, & Kuhl, 1999). This is the basis of wanting to belong. Identification may be the most common and possibly the most positive way of belonging as children get older. For some children, identifying with a group or team may occur only in a classroom.

The methods of putting teams together are numerous. The only one I object to is letting students choose their own teams. Most of us have been in that humiliating situation when we were picked last or—what could be worse?—no one wanted us! Assemble the teams yourself, or if you wish, you may put them together randomly. This team is for identification, not for a specific project. It gives the students a group to be with as they enter the room.

When I take attendance, I say, "If you have 100 percent of your team members seated and ready to go, raise your hand, and say 'Yes!'" They have to check and make sure that their teammates are present. It gives kids a good feeling to know that people are going to notice if they aren't there. Team members might help each other with homework, remind each other of upcoming assignments, and keep each other on task.

> Teams promote social skills. Getting along with different types of people is essential in this world of team-oriented business.

Teams promote social skills. Getting along with different types of people is essential in this world of team-oriented business. Follow some simple steps to give your teams an identity.

1. *Give the teams some questions to answer as a get-to-know-each-other activity.* We sometimes assume that kids have gone to school together long enough to know each other, but some questions can rouse some interesting conversation and bits of information they didn't know before. Use questions such as, "Who are three people you would like to have over for dinner tonight?" Or "Who would you like to see walk in the door right now?" Or "If you could be anywhere else right now, where would you be?"

2. *Have the teams pick a team name.* Students are used to identifying sports teams with names, so this may be fun. Make sure they keep the names positive, and if you like, they may be associated with a specific topic. Using the analogy of the Wizard of Oz, I have assembled teams and assigned each member the name of a character from the story (see Table 5.3). The character has specific tasks to take care of for the team. What I find compelling about this strategy is the ability to quickly get students to accomplish specific tasks. For instance, I may say, "Okay, I need all of the Dorothys to come up and count out enough assignment sheets for the team."

Table 5.3   Teams Composed of Wizard of Oz Characters

Character	Responsibility
Dorothy	**Team Leader:** Attendance, homework assignments for absences
Cowardly Lion	**Risk-Taker:** Asks questions for the team
Tin Man	**Emotional Coach:** Motivates and helps control impulsivity
Scarecrow	**Informer:** Investigates, explains, researches
Toto	**Mascot:** In charge of team logo

3. *How about some team colors?* Or a team handshake? Or a team logo? Talking about these will bring the group together and help make them a team.

4. *Have your teams make up a cheer or pick a theme song.* This helps with the identification process, can be loads of fun, and you can have them use the cheer or song to notify you when their team has completed an assignment or project.

5. *Team goals may be appropriate now.* What do these team members have in common as goals? Will they help each other reach them? Are they attainable? When? Many teams need help setting limits and being specific with goals.

6. *Do you want a team scorecard or chart for self-assessment?* This could be a simple 8½″ × 11″ sheet of paper or a larger piece of construction paper (see Table 5.4). Team members could assess themselves on cooperation, participation, punctuality, and homework completion. These are only examples. Be creative!

Table 5.4   Team Chart Sample

Mrs. Sprenger's Team Chart, 3rd Period	Cooperation	Participation	Punctuality	Homework	Average
The Dendrites	5	7	10	8	7.5
The Brainiacs	7	9	9	8	8.3
The Dreamers	6	7	10	9	8.0
The Thinkers	9	10	9	10	9.5

7. *If you want team leaders, rather than have students vote for one, let each person decide if he or she wants to be a leader.* Perhaps they can take turns. Give them your job description for team leader so they know what will be expected. If no team members are interested in the leadership position, you may choose a leader and try to work with that student to bring out leadership qualities. Try to choose a student who already has some good emotional intelligence skills or someone who works well with others. You may be surprised at how well some students do in this capacity. Often, leadership skills are not expressed because students have not been in situations to use them. This may be a great opportunity to discuss world or local leaders and how they conduct themselves. Perhaps the students could pick one of these well-known and successful leaders to model themselves after.

Now you have a team! These kids have goals, criteria to assess themselves as good team members, a chance at leadership, a name for identification, and a cheer or song for fun! If this sounds like a lengthy process, it needn't be. Don't allow much time for these steps. Show them that working together makes work go faster and easier.

Teams cannot stay together for long periods of time. As in any social situation, at some point, a hierarchy will develop, and that means some students are going to end up at the bottom of the social structure. You don't want to leave them there for very long, so shuffle teams often enough to avoid this. Remember, this is a base team, and you can mix them up for other projects, activities, and subjects. For this reason, I find it imperative to continually have Get-to-know-each-other activities on a regular basis. Sometimes I do it in pairs or teams, and sometimes whole-class participation is necessary. The more the students know about each other and themselves, the better they get along in any group situation. I have included several activities in Figure 5.2.

Delaying Gratification

Why not try your own marshmallow test? Depending on the grade level you teach, you wouldn't necessarily use marshmallows. This might be a good way to show your students what impulse control is all about. Discuss impulses and how difficult it can be to wait for things. Ask your students for examples of situations where they have difficulty being patient.

This is a good time to talk about their goals again. Achieving those goals may very well be related to impulse control. Talk about their personal goals that are unrelated to school. Are they saving for a new bike? A new computer game? How about eating healthier food and staying away from sweets? Explain how

Figure 5.2   Activities for Teams or Classmates to Get to Know Each Other

1. *Get-to-Know-Each-Other Sheet.* The tried and true tactic, with boxes for students to sign (wears glasses, likes the color blue, reads mysteries, etc.). Create one after your students have filled out an index card with information about themselves, and include something from each person's card.

2. *Venn Diagram.* Find a partner and create a Venn diagram with the similarities and differences of the two of you. Have each member of a pair introduce the other.

3. *What Do We Have in Common?* Have students move their chairs into a circle with no spaces between chairs. You stand in the center and introduce yourself. Then say something about yourself. Anyone who has the same thing in common must get up and move to another open seat. The person in the center tries to get a seat as well. This leaves one person in the center to continue the game. This is great fun and students discover fascinating commonalities (somewhat like Musical Chairs).

4. *To Tell the Truth.* Each person writes down two true statements about him- or herself and one false statement. They take turns reading their statements to the team, and the teammates guess which one is false.

5. *Who in the Room?* On a flip chart, write four or five categories. Give students each a card, and have them write the numerals 1 through 5 along the left margin. Then they must go around the room and get signatures of those who fit categories you designate as 1 through 5. For instance, these might include *has more than one pet, has traveled out of the country, has read* The Adventures of Tom Sawyer *(or some suitable novel), has more than two siblings, has been to a rodeo,* etc.

6. *What's My Line?* Give students a few minutes to think of a famous person. In their teams, they play a 20-questions type of game with only yes or no answers until they guess the famous person.

7. *Charming Charmin.* Take a roll of toilet paper into class. Hand the roll to the first person you see in class, and tell that person to take as many sheets as he or she likes and then pass the roll to another student. When all students have their sheets, explain that they all have to tell one thing about themselves for each sheet they tore off. This is fun!

this skill can affect their lives as they make decisions to pursue careers. I use the example with my students of my master's degree. I had the opportunity to delay my first job and work on the degree, but I couldn't resist the money I would be making if I took the job. As I look back on that decision, I wish I had worked toward the degree then, before I had children and other responsibilities that made it more difficult.

After your students have an understanding of the concept, help them delay gratification. Ask them to finish certain projects or assignments before they do something frivolous and fun. Talk to them about doing their homework after school before they turn on the computer or the television. Paying attention in class has a great deal to do with impulse control. Remind those who have difficulty that you are asking them to refrain from talking or drawing until you have finished the lesson.

Choices

This is one of the basic needs often mentioned by the experts. Students need to feel that they have some control in their lives. That also relates to school, which is a large part of what they do each day. You do not lose any control by offering students choices in the types of projects they create, in the types of assessments you give them, or even in the topics you cover. Within limits, students can make these choices.

You can also bring in the opportunity to delay gratification with this technique. Tell your students that the curriculum requires that they study both fiction and nonfiction. Which would they like to cover first? Do they want what they consider to be the most fun first?—or would they like to save the best for last?

> **Students need to feel that they have some control in their lives.**

An important component of emotional intelligence is making the right choice when dealing with your own emotions and with the emotions of others. Explain to your students that the choices they make may influence feelings and behaviors.

Rapport Skills

Here's something we all want to have, but we rarely think of teaching it to our students. I have enjoyed teaching the basics to my sixth, seventh, and eighth graders, and I believe that one can begin to learn these skills at any age.

Explain to the students that having rapport with another person does not have to mean that they are friends with them. Rapport skills just help them get along with everyone. I usually begin by talking to them about how they approach me when they want something. Does it make sense to ask me a question when I am talking to someone else? When I approach them and stand over them at their desks, are they comfortable? Would they be more comfortable if I were to sit in the desk beside them and speak to them on their level? Do they like it when their parents ask them to do something while their favorite television show is on?

To us, as educators, this all seems to be common sense. It's not. It's emotional and social intelligence. Below, I list some basic rapport skills. It's fun to have the kids practice these while they role-play and as a team activity.

Steps to Build Rapport

1. Listen to others carefully. We all want to feel that our words and ideas are important. If necessary, repeat back to them what they said in your own words. Make sure you understand their meaning.

2. Match the other person physically. If Mom is sitting down, sit down beside her and speak on her level.

3. Match the other person's volume and tonality. If your friend is whispering, whisper back (unless you're in my class and are not supposed to be talking at all!).

4. Seek the other person's opinion. We all like to think that our thoughts and feelings are important.

5. Try to find something to agree on. If your new teammate doesn't like sports, try shopping. Ask questions until you find a common ground.

6. Sit beside persons whom you must confront. Sitting across from them separates you. If you are next to them, they feel you're on their side.

Books on the subject include *Instant Rapport* by Michael Brooks (1989). Faber and Mazlish (1995) share similar ideas in *How to Talk So Kids Can Learn.* There is also the old standby that is not used often enough—*How to Win Friends and Influence People* by Dale Carnegie (1936). These are all listed in the reference section.

Journaling

This technique is an easy way for students to start recognizing their feelings. It can be helpful to give them just a few minutes at the beginning of class to write whatever they may be thinking about. This may also clear the air for some who enter class with emotional issues that would interfere with their learning. If their amygdalae are in charge of their brains, I know I will not be getting information into any of their memory lanes. Emotions must always be dealt with first (Sprenger, 1999, 2005). Sometimes, they may ask for ideas to get started. Journal suggestions may be found in books, but I like to afford older students the opportunity to just write.

This task may be easier for your more verbal students, but it is great practice in writing for all students. Decide from the beginning whether you are going to read their journals. Some years, I tell my students that I will read them only if there are entries they would like me to read. Other years, I have collected journals and written short notes back to students. They really enjoyed this technique, but when I have 160 to 200 students a day, it takes too much time. There have been especially tense days when my students spent more time writing than I spent teaching. For instance, after some of the school shootings and terrorist attacks that have taken place, it was necessary for many students to get their feelings out. Some could talk about it, but others needed to write. Just five minutes of journaling can improve the makeup of the entire period. This takes us back to the idea of control. Writing about an experience gives the student a feeling of control over the situation (Restak, 2000).

When I have had the opportunity to read my students' journals, I have learned much more about them than I would have otherwise. I have discovered who has special interests, such as stamp collecting and astronomy. Some of those topics don't readily come up during the day. It has given me an opportunity to speak to students about things that are important to them, and I have sometimes been able to bring up the topics in class discussions in case they want to share their interests.

Physical Outlets

As stated in Chapter 1, having physical outlets is an important and basic need. Your classroom need not become a racetrack or a wrestling mat for healthy movement to take place. Exercise reduces stress, causes the neurotransmitters that enhance learning to be produced, increases our heart and pulmonary functions, and can be a lot of fun!

What kind of physical outlets are possible in your classroom?

Math

When children are learning measurement, instead of measuring small objects that fit on the desk, expand the range to include large objects so that children have to get up and move while measuring. How tall is the chalkboard? What is its area? How many feet (your own) does it take to get from your desk to the door? Horses are measured by hands—how many hands high is the file cabinet?

How about going outside for math? Finding geometric shapes outdoors can be fun and energizing for your students. A lot of emotions can be shared on these "field trips." Children can travel with their teams or partners and learn to cooperate as they do the assignment.

Science

Lab work is physical, but it usually employs only small motor movement. Larger movement is what you are after. Using the outdoors is great in nice weather. Leaf collecting, bug collecting, identifying clouds and drawing them, picking up rocks, identifying types of trees, and discussing ecology can be done outside. Inside? A science teacher in my building sent her students through the building to identify transparent, translucent, and opaque glass. They were up, moving, and learning. Bones and body parts can be labeled and identified using students themselves as the models. This promotes movement, learning, and fun.

Are you talking about weather? Become the weather. If you were a hurricane, how would you move? A tornado? A calm breeze? What does rain sound like? Make that noise with your body. What about a thunderstorm?

Social Studies

Reenactments are good for physical outlets. Divide the room in half into North and South for the Civil War. Act out a battle, a court case, or a presidential debate and put on costumes. This will enhance memory for the events in addition to providing movement.

Even I got bored when I taught geography and we covered latitude and longitude. But when the students lay on the ground representing the lines, the class and the concept came to life. Someone always asked, "Can I be the prime meridian today?"

Literature

Role-playing provides physical outlets for many children. There are numerous opportunities to role-play scenes from stories and plays. Putting poetry into movement is more challenging and sometimes more fun. Having students create their own skits or plays affords plenty of movement as they prepare scenery and props, practice for the performance, and add music and dance to their creation.

Role-playing provides physical outlets for many children.

Grammar and Writing

Until I discovered a method of teaching grammar that allowed for oral recitation, jingles, and movement, I was quite low in the physical department in English class. I could get kids to stand up as parts of speech and have them scramble to make sentences. They enjoyed that, but I couldn't do that very often and keep it fresh.

Taking their writing and making a reader's theater from it works well. Many students can be involved in this type of production. Charades is another way to provide a physical outlet. Other word games are also physical and exciting.

What about simply adding movement to your classes on a daily basis? You can call it exercise or stretching. You can turn on the "Hokey Pokey" or the "Chicken Dance" and promote movement that way. The National Dance Association encourages us to include dance in our classes. Incorporating modern dance into academic presentations gives students the opportunity to work on spatial and kinesthetic skills (Mann, 1999).

We know that movement helps build a better brain. In her book, *Smart Moves*, Carla Hannaford (2005) provides wonderful information on the importance of movement as it pertains to learning. She includes many of the exercises and movements from *Brain Gym*, by Paul and Gail Dennison (1994). Many teachers feel that these exercises are the way to start each class period and believe it makes a huge difference in the atmosphere of their classrooms. I have never been disappointed when I have used movement as part of my teaching activities, and if I can't incorporate it into whatever I am teaching—there's always Chubby Checker's "Twist and Shout!"

YOU GOTTA HAVE HEART, BUT WHAT ABOUT GUTS?

In this case I am referring to more than having the nerve to do something. New research supports the importance of feelings in motivation, learning, and making decisions. That gut response is actually a chemical reaction from your amygdala and then some added thought from your neocortex. In other words, emotions are part of rationality (Goleman et al., 2002).

Consider the test questions in Figure 5.3. As you figure out the answers to each question, take note of how your brain is working. For the first question, you can feel your head thinking as you go through the words to define them or see what is familiar. The second question stirs your emotions, and it feels quite different. You must use your emotional intelligence for the second question. (The answer to #1 is letter *e*; the answer to #2 could vary on any given day, but the emotional intelligence coaches would want us to choose letter *c*.) Researcher Simon Baron-Cohen (Johnson, 2004) and his team have whittled down the number of emotions we seem to have to a mere 412! It just makes sense that we would utilize those as we go about our daily activities of learning, remembering, and making decisions.

Do you remember being told in school that your first answer to a question is probably the correct one? Three out of four times it is. It's that gut reaction that we rely on—the answer feels right!

How many times do we use this intuition as teachers? How about the time a student turned in a paper and you knew (with no proof) that it wasn't his or her work? Or you look at standardized test scores of your students and you know that some were just having a bad day and the score is not indicative of their achievement? Of course, you can use the facts you have about the students to defend your decisions, but it was your first thought or feeling about the data that helped you come to the conclusions.

Figure 5.3   Intelligence Tests: IQ or EQ

---

1. Which of the following is not a characteristic of a lion?
   a. Has skin hanging down from its belly to protect it when getting kicked
   b. Roars loud enough to be heard for five miles
   c. Is about 11 feet long
   d. Sleeps over 20 hours a day
   e. Is both carnivorous and herbivorous

2. You are walking down the hall at school. You start to trip but regain your balance. Two students are walking the other way and they giggle. You
   a. pretend that there is something wrong with the floor in the hallway, and call a custodian.
   b. give the students a dirty look.
   c. smile and continue down the hall.
   d. stop and write the students a detention.
   e. throw your grade book at the students.

HEARTBEAT

I am pleased to say that since the first edition of this book was published, the world has become more aware of the power of emotions. CASEL, the Collaborative for Academic, Social, and Emotional Learning, has a list titled, "Essential Skills for Academic and Social-Emotional Learning." The list includes *know yourself and others, make responsible decisions, care for others,* and *know how to act* (Elias & Arnold, 2006).

Researchers have found that prosocial behavior in the classroom is associated with positive intellectual results and is predictive of performance on standardized achievement tests (Zins, Weissberg, Wang, & Walberg, 2004).

Many educators are test driven and find that working with emotional intelligence skills takes up too much of their time. Like the Tin Man, your students want to have a heart. They also want someone to recognize and acknowledge that heart in them. Only in this way can their journey down the Yellow Brick Road lead them to the cognitive skills they need to feel successful and accomplished. The Tin Man had a heart all along, as he finally learned when others acknowledged his feelings and he acknowledged them himself. Do that for your students, and make the journey fulfilling for all of you.

We're Off to See . . .

Now that we have looked at some of the research and strategies on emotions, our next stop is to consider cognitive approaches. Modalities, multiple intelligences, and cognitive growth are areas to consider when taking students from sensory input to higher levels of thinking.

WIZDOM

Key Points to Ponder

1. Emotional intelligence can raise test scores.

2. Emotional intelligence is learned through observation and interaction.

3. There are specific strategies that can raise EQ.

Suggestions

- Keep a close eye on the hierarchies of your teams. Try a technique such as a jigsaw occasionally to make all team members feel important. To jigsaw, divide material into parts (chunks of information, sections, vocabulary words, etc.). Give each team member a different bit of information. Have members from each team who are assigned the same information work together to discuss and learn the new information until they become experts on it. Then, have the experts return to their teams and teach the information to the team. Each member is an expert in a different area, and all areas are important. Every team member, therefore, is important (Fogarty, 2001).
- Combining rapport skills with role-play can be very effective.
- Your enthusiasm and encouragement can make many strategies successful. Emotions are contagious. It is vital that you raise your own emotional intelligence level in order to model the EQ strategies for your students.

6 If I Only Had a Brain

From Sensory Input to Higher Levels of Thinking

If you will come to me tomorrow morning, I will stuff your head with brains. I cannot tell you how to use them, however; you must find that out for yourself.

—The Wizard

A low humming emanates from my classroom. As I approach the door with a teacher from a nearby school, I pray that things are under control. After all, this teacher came to see a brain-compatible classroom in action. Did I say action? I mean a brain-based classroom where children are getting beyond stress and using emotion to motivate themselves toward higher-order thinking. Yes, that's what I hope she sees when she enters my room. Not too much action—I don't want to see Trent throwing erasers and Jay tossing spit wads. This happened once when I left the room at the beginning of the year, and I still have nightmares about it.

We enter: I am tentative and hopeful; she is curious and perhaps a little skeptical. The humming is louder when we enter. I allow my guest to go first and I pause at the door to get a full view of the room. It is amazing! Howard Gardner would be proud! That hum represents the low buzz of seventh-grade voices as they work diligently on their projects. Most never realized that I had left the room, and others are still unaware of my return. Our ritual for greeting guests is to stand and applaud. (This either makes them feel welcome or keeps them from ever coming back. It also avoids feelings of being disrupted—we have a duty to perform, and we do it, as one of our rituals.)

The state of flow abounds. The amount of teamwork and the quality of the projects mesmerize the visiting teacher as the students work in an almost pulsing fashion to stay synchronized. Some may call this synergy; others may call it flow. I just call it the way things should be when children's needs are met, the task is challenging, and the skills are in place. It is the optimal state of learning: I know what the problem is, I know there is an answer to the problem, and I have the tools to find that answer.

The visiting teacher smiles and asks if she can walk around and ask questions. I encourage her to observe. I ask her to refrain from breaking the flow and, instead, wait for students to offer their expertise. I do encourage her to ask the students if they know what it is they are trying to learn. Can they tell her what our goal is? She does. They do. Life is good.

Is this the way it is every day in my classroom? I would love to say yes, but it wouldn't be true. Does this happen more and more often as I become more aware of what it takes to have a brain-compatible atmosphere? Yes. How do I begin to get to this point? Just as you read in the preceding chapters, I have to work on de-stressing first and then on emotional intelligence. I cannot get my students using higher-order thinking and creativity until we have reached this point. The most important job I have is to manage my classroom in a manner that is conducive to higher levels of thought and creativity.

> **How do I get to this point? I have to work on de-stressing first and then on emotional intelligence.**

This all sounds pretty good, but what about children at different age levels? Where are they in their brain development? And if they are de-stressed and emotionally aware, what cognitive skills can they perform?

COGNITIVE SKILLS

Kindergarten and Grades 1 and 2

We must continually keep in mind that students in all grades are at varying levels of brain development. There are no absolutes, but a wide variety of developmental skills can be addressed. From ages four to seven, the right cerebral hemisphere is developing more rapidly than the left. This means that most children are better kinesthetically. They are spontaneous, use a lot of emotion, and are usually quite good at imaging. Neuropsychologists refer to a "five-to-seven shift" as the brain goes through so many changes. From ages seven to nine, we see more development in the left cerebral hemisphere. Now, language skills are better. Sentence structure and syntax are developing as are spelling skills. Students become more aware of the details, whereas earlier, they were seeing more of the big picture. Growth in sensory association areas of the brain allows for more flexible communication between modalities. Now children are more able to read for meaning and listen to sentences being dictated and write them down (Healy, 2004).

At this level, we are definitely into concrete operations with the beginnings of moving to abstractions. These children do best with hands-on activities. Social interaction is just beginning. Students are still very *me* oriented. Because of a slight difference in the hemispheres between girls and boys, girls tend to have better verbal skills and boys seem to excel spatially. Fine motor skills are still a challenge to many students in these grades, but boys especially are displaying more gross movements.

Grades 3, 4, and 5

Students are still in concrete operations in these grades. There are signs of abstract thinking at basic levels. It is time to offer more options as far as learning and assessment are concerned. Some of these students will be capable of more in-depth research with some synthesis and analysis included. Others will still be very hands-on and will need opportunities to share their knowledge in more tactile ways.

At this stage, the quest for learning is strong. Children enjoy seeking out information and may want to act as reporters or interviewers. Peers are extremely important to students of this age, although the teacher has enormous influence over children. To use both strong adult and peer influence calls for working in large groups with the teacher as coach. By Grade 5, students begin to empathize with large groups as they develop more world and cultural knowledge. Thus it is possible to use their emotional intelligence to encourage research about issues that affect communities of people (Wood, 2005).

Grades 6, 7, and 8

Typically, we are dealing with the middle school child at this stage. These students are coordinating social relations, surging hormones, and a search for personal identity. During this time, students are concerned with the concept of fairness. In their minds, sameness and fairness must be identical, and this issue is sensitive and important to handle. Physical development is beginning to accelerate, and there are gross differences in development leading to even more delicate situations.

During this time, students are concerned with the concept of fairness.

The brain is undergoing some enormous changes that may continue through the high school years. At puberty, a girl's hypothalamus begins to secrete chemicals to increase appetite. This is nature's way of preparing the body for childbirth by adding fat. In our society, however, this may be cause for alarm, and many girls become obsessed with their weight. The amygdalae in both boys and girls enlarge at this time due to the release of testosterone. This hormone is more prevalent in males. Their amygdalae become larger than those of the females, which may cause overemotional reactions. At the same time, the hippocampus, which we know is a strong memory system for factual information, grows from the release of estrogen. Estrogen is more prevalent in females, so they have larger hippocampi. To put the consequences of this simply, we have children beginning adolescence. The boys may be overemotional and overreactive due to the size and sensitivity of the emotional structure, the amygdala. The girls, who may have an easier time remembering factual information, could also be struggling with their body images as their appetites increase (Brownlee, 1999).

If that sounds difficult to handle, there happens to be more. The prefrontal cortex is the area of the cerebrum that controls the amygdala. It has not yet fully developed and may not do so until these students are in their 20s. Consequently, the brain structure that could help these young adults deal with their problems may not be physically able to do so. We may just have to accept the fact that these students may have difficulty making good choices (Walsh, 2004). Our expectations of them may also be too high. They may not be able to handle the higher-order thinking that we assume they can. That is, jumping to abstract work may be difficult for some. Therefore, concrete learning followed by the abstract may make a big difference.

That was the bad news. The good news is that the brain is plastic. It is also still growing and changing. It is not too late for positive transformations, and eventually, most of these students will have the physical ability to perform the operations that are expected of adults.

Let's take a closer look at those very specialized and important brain areas, the prefrontal cortices. Why are they so important? Why do they affect so many skills, talents, and behaviors? There are two important functions. First, this structure acts as logical decision maker in the brain. As the amygdala creates an emotional attitude toward people and events, the prefrontal cortex shapes that attitude or stops it from being displayed. As Dr. David Walsh (2004) states, "Adolescent brains get the gas before they get the brakes." Without the prefrontal cortex, decision making relies heavily on a strictly emotional response. The other function of this area is working memory. For information to be processed—that is, new information worked with and added to

> As the amygdala creates an emotional attitude toward people and events, the prefrontal cortex shapes that attitude or stops it from being displayed.

old information or old information spread out and reworked—there has to be space for this to occur. The prefrontal cortex is the working space for these processes.

Sasha and Rochelle are studying for a final exam in Spanish. They are working at Sasha's house because her little brother is gone for the evening, and Rochelle's house is always crowded and noisy with all her siblings and their friends. The girls spread their books and notes out on Sasha's bed. Rochelle opens her text and begins to compare her notes and the chapter contents. Sasha goes to the radio and turns it on.

"Could you please turn down that music?" Rochelle asks, with some frustration in her voice.

"Oh, this is the song that was playing when Angelo and I were on our first date!" Sasha declares.

"I don't care when it was playing—it ain't playing now!" Rochelle suddenly snaps the radio off.

"What's the matter with you? This is my house, and I can listen to whatever I want! Besides, it will be over in a minute, and then we'll study!"

"You can study by yourself!" With that, Rochelle grabs her books and storms out of the house.

In this case, Rochelle was reacting emotionally. She may have been stressed about the exam and then became further irritated by the music while she was trying to concentrate. She overreacted to the situation; it appeared that Sasha would turn off the radio right after the song. Rochelle was having trouble controlling her emotional response to the situation. Her prefrontal cortex was not able to monitor her amygdala's response to the circumstances.

Nathan could not sit still. It was only one class period until art class, and he could not wait to get his hands on Michael. If Michael thought for one minute that he could get away with saying that kind of stuff about his baby sister, well, boy, he was gonna get it. Nathan watched the clock as the minutes ticked by. He wanted to jump up and run out of English and go find Michael, but something wouldn't let him do it. He looked up at Mr. Sterling's algebra equation, but he had no clue as to what was going on. He tried to concentrate on what his teacher was explaining, but he couldn't stop thinking about those words Michael had said, "Nathan's little sister is easy—anybody can be with her!" Thinking those words took Nathan's breath away. He wiggled in his seat and tried to focus on the board again. Finally, the bell rang, and Nathan headed for the door.

"Oh, Nathan," Mr. Sterling called to him, "don't forget that assignment."

"Oh, yeah, sure!" Nathan yelled back. But he didn't know what Mr. Sterling was talking about.

> Nathan was fortunate that his prefrontal cortex was able to control his emotions. As much as he wanted to act on his need to find Michael, he knew he should wait until his next class with him. Unfortunately, because the prefrontal cortex was so busy keeping his amygdala in check, Nathan had no space free for working memory. He couldn't take any of the information that was offered in his math class and work with it in his head. He didn't even realize that he had been given an assignment.

Like the Scarecrow who was looking for the brain he really already had, adolescents sometimes address the same issue. The brain is there, but the awareness is not.

Grades 9, 10, 11, and 12

Much of what was just described goes on through the high school level. There are some significant differences in the progress of this growth at all of the levels. Students in ninth grade may not be as capable of abstract work as most twelfth graders. At this stage of development, students begin to hang out in smaller groups. The physical body is rapidly maturing, and many of these students have the cerebral capabilities to plan for the future. They are still dealing with fluctuating hormones as the matter of sex becomes an issue. Estrogen and testosterone levels vary daily as well as seasonally.

At this stage of development, students begin to hang out in smaller groups.

Studies have compared teenagers with adults in various emotional situations. Using the brain-imaging technique called **magnetic resonance imaging (MRI)**, researchers have discovered that most adults use their prefrontal cortices to make decisions, whereas teenagers still rely heavily on their amygdalae (Dana Alliance for Brain Initiatives, 1998).

Dr. Jay Giedd has ongoing studies of the adolescent brain. Using fMRI, functional magnetic resonance imaging, that shows structure and function, he regularly scans the brains of adolescents. He says, "Teenagers are capable of enormous intellectual and artistic accomplishments, but the basic part of the brain that gives us strategies and organizing and perhaps warns us of potential consequences is not fully on board yet" (Weinberger, Elvevag, & Giedd, 2005).

The first knowledge of the importance of the frontal lobes came from a situation that occurred in 1848. A man named Phineas Gage was a foreman for a railroad company. Explosives were used to clear away boulders and debris to lay down track. Phineas had the responsibility of using a tamping rod (an iron rod, pointed at one end, about three feet long) to compress the explosives into a hole. As Phineas was tamping, the explosives went off accidentally. The explosion sent the iron rod through Phineas' left eye socket, through his frontal lobes, and out through the top of his head. The tamping rod landed 30 meters behind him. Amazingly, Phineas never lost consciousness. He got back on his feet by himself and was helped to a nearby doctor's office. After several weeks, Phineas was released by the doctor and sent home.

As amazing as his ability to recover had been, changes began to take place in Phineas. A well-liked, mild-mannered person suddenly turned into a rude and crude individual. He could not get along with others because he could not control his emotional outbursts. Phineas lost his job, his wife, and his family. He lived for another 13 years, at which time he began to have seizures and eventually died. The medical community was astonished that Phineas still had many intellectual capacities, language, and memory. The extraordinary functions of the frontal lobes began to be examined after this incident. Researchers found that the remarkable area that controls impulsivity and emotional stability is the prefrontal cortex, the last area of the brain to fully develop (Shimamura, 2000).

Higher-order thinking may be expected of many teenagers and should be offered to all, but we must always keep in mind that development of this critical area will vary. That prefrontal cortex may not be fully developed until the mid or late 20s. Differing degrees of acceleration are possible, and students need choices in their study and assessments. Patience and understanding are key here, because some students will have more difficulty than others using abstract reasoning and good decision making (Weinberger et al., 2005).

PROMOTING COGNITIVE GROWTH

The Scarecrow didn't know he had it all: courage, heart, and brains. Once children know that they are capable of learning, and their brains are ready to learn, the next step is for the teacher to decide what kind of approach to take to teach them. In my classroom, I work hard to keep three areas in mind as I create not only lessons but also an atmosphere for learning. I begin by helping students understand how they learn best. I then create every unit of study while keeping in mind how memory works. If memory is our only evidence of learning, conscious effort must be put into creating those memories. Finally, I try to keep the multiple intelligences in mind as I create a classroom for learners with diverse gifts and resources.

> If memory is our only evidence of learning, conscious effort must be put into creating those memories.

Understanding How to Learn

I was studying for my comprehensive exams for my master's degree. My friend had suggested that I take the questions the head of the department had given us to study and record them and the answers on cassette tapes. This way, I could listen to them in the car on my way to school and back. It seemed to be a good idea. I made the first tape with the answer I had chosen and started my daily ritual of playing it. I was impressed with the amount of time I was putting into my "studying." It was a great way to get two things done at once, which immediately made me feel that I was putting my time to good use.

By the end of the week, I thought I was ready. I sat down at the computer with the first question; I was ready to type all that I had learned in the car. My hands were poised at the keyboard as I read the question over and over from the top of the screen. It suddenly dawned on me that I couldn't remember what I had recorded on that tape player. Angrily, I stood up and stomped out of the room. How dumb could I be? Had I really not been paying attention to that tape? Surely, two or three hours of listening should have placed something in my memory banks.

I threw those tapes away and began studying the way I had always studied. I looked up the questions (again) and wrote down the answers in my notebook. I read over those notes each night, underlining and highlighting the phrases I needed to remember. A week later, I sat at the computer again. This time my success was assured. I had done exactly what I had needed to do for the learner that I am. I had visual representations of the answers to those questions in my mind. I could even remember the page numbers and the places on the pages for some of my information. Obviously, the friendly advice I had received came from an auditory learner. She also did quite well on the comps—and had only listened to tapes.

Noted researchers Rita and Ken Dunn, of St. John's University in New York, have done extensive studies on the way people learn. They believe that there are three strong sensory channels for learning: visual, auditory, and kinesthetic (Rose & Nicholl, 1997). Although some refer to a learning modality as a preference, others refer to it as a strength (Guild & Garger, 1998). I believe it is a little of both. We use the networks of neurons that solve our problems for us in the easiest and fastest way. As we continue to use those same neurons, the connections become stronger. Therefore, if an auditory learner gets positive results from listening and dialoguing, he or she will continue to do so as a preference, and that modality will be strengthened through use. According to

> We use the networks of neurons that solve our problems for us in the easiest and fastest way.

neurophysiologist Dr. Carla Hannaford (2005), not honoring a student's unique learning style causes stress that can limit frontal lobe development.

I have found in my classroom that determining a student's preferred modality is helpful. I also find it necessary to teach to all three modalities to reach all my students. In some cases, this can be challenging, but most of the time it takes very little planning to allow for all preferences. Table 6.1 gives you a quick overview of the characteristics of each modality.

Visual Learners

These students are happiest when they can see the information I am sharing. They absorb the world through words and pictures. They may not hear what you're saying, but they see what you mean! This type of learner can be divided into two subtypes: visual and print-oriented. Those who are print-oriented tend to think with words and take in information better with words than pictures. They may express themselves best the same way. Neil Fleming, a New Zealand researcher, calls his learning style method VARK. It stands for visual, auditory, reading/writing, and kinesthetic. Although I have not used his materials, they look rather interesting and you may want to visit his Web site at http://www.vark-learn.com/english/page.asp?p=whatsnew. The idea of print orientation has been around for a very long time, but the VARK package offers us another option for approaching learning styles.

Table 6.1   Characteristics of the Three Modalities

Visual Learner	Auditory Learner	Kinesthetic Learner
Sees the world through pictures or words	Talks as much as listens	Wiggles and jiggles
Sits up straight to see	Prefers oral reports to written ones	Prefers hands-on learning and whole body learning
Usually in the front of the class . . . doesn't want to miss anything!	Books on tape are sometimes helpful	Is sometimes content with drawing
Appreciates charts, maps, graphs, handouts, and video clips	Often good with dialects and accents	Likes movement and actions
Is often upset by clutter	May run off on tangents	Bells and whistles on items are of interest
Often visually organized	Needs no eye contact	May not hear what you say or see what you mean
Can see in his or her mind	Talks to self	Movement turns on this brain
	Distracted easily by noises	

It is not difficult to teach visual learners because we have overhead projectors, chalkboards, textbooks, handouts, and posters to help convey the message. Some of these learners want to see me solve the problem to understand it, and others need to read about it for full comprehension. Visual learners may be offended when you read to them from the text or from the overhead; however, reading may help others with different modality preferences.

Visual learners absorb the world through pictures and words.

Visual memory has often been thought to be the strongest kind of memory, but we shall see later that rote memory may well be much stronger. To a visual learner, a picture may be worth a thousand words, or those thousand words may help this student create a beautiful picture of his or her own.

As a visual learner, I create scenes as I listen to music to help myself remember the words and the meaning. When music videos became popular, I was truly offended that someone else was trying to create my pictures for me. It took the personalization away from me, and I found it frustrating.

Visual learners often sit in the front of the classroom and often sit up very straight. They don't want to miss seeing anything. They also have a tendency to watch the teacher. It makes me feel very good to have students so entranced while I am teaching. In fact, in my early days of teaching, I found myself teaching to these students who seemed to be so interested. As I gained more experience and started using the modalities, I realized that this kind of student would stay with me without more visual acknowledgment—and that the other learners who were not looking might need my attention more.

Auditory Learners

Auditory learners learn by talking and listening. They enjoy having something read aloud to them or explained to them. Information isn't real to them until they have had a chance to discuss it. Looking at the teacher is not important to them, so I may find them looking out the window while I am speaking. This used to bother me a great deal, because I thought they were daydreaming. Now I know that I just have to check in with them to be sure they are keeping up with the information—and they usually are. Those who have this modality preference would rather give you an oral book report, and you may not see much written down in a written report.

When these students read text, and sometimes they don't, you will often see them moving their lips or mumbling. In fact, these learners have a tendency to talk to themselves. If you are with them on a day when they haven't had much verbal intercourse, you may find their banter quite tiring. Of course, these auditory learners expect you to remember what they tell you even though they often have to repeat information to themselves several times to remember it. Dialects come easily to many auditory learners. They often do very well with foreign languages. Asking them to sit still and be quiet for long periods of time may be quite difficult. They may be extremely sound sensitive and easily disturbed by noises such as the radiator kicking on, others chewing gum, or the simple clicking of a pen. They usually enjoy music but may have their concentration interrupted by music they are unfamiliar with.

Auditory memory is sometimes stored in an unusual fashion, as though the information is on a cassette tape. These students have to rewind and fast-forward to find information that is not asked for in the order in which it was stored. Think of the alphabet. Most of us learned it to the tune of "Twinkle, Twinkle, Little Star." Those letters are stored in our cerebellum in order and to a rhythm. It is sometimes difficult to answer a question such as "What letter comes before H?" Often, one has to run through the song to get to that answer. Auditory learners encounter that problem on a test when the questions are not in the same order in which the material was presented. These listeners may turn their heads from side to side as they are trying to pick up sounds. They can sometimes be spotted tapping out beats on their knees or on their desks. They don't have to sit up straight like the visual learners because sight is not very important to them (Grinder, 1991).

Kinesthetic Learners

Kinesthetic learners have probably had the most difficulties in our traditional classrooms. Rows of chairs, sitting still, and being quiet do not allow these students' brains to become activated. One very bright student, Erin, is this type of learner and had many difficulties throughout elementary and high school. She is now a junior in college, and her parents and I are both grateful that she stuck with the system, as hard as it was for her. When writing my previous books and discussing modalities, I often asked Erin questions

Kinesthetic learners have difficulty in the traditional classroom.

about her classes. How does it feel to be a kinesthetic learner in a visual and auditory world? "It's simple to explain to you," she said. "Walk into a totally dark room and try to read." I realized that I would not be able to learn anything under those conditions. What did Erin do in those "dark days" of traditional classrooms?

Kinesthetic learners need hands-on activities. They need movement. If they are reading a story, they hope for action and pay more attention to the action than to the description of scenery or characters. These students gesture a lot. To memorize, they often walk with the information in their hands. Erin walked back and forth in the back of my classroom. She never disturbed anyone, and it allowed her to pay attention. She was an excellent student.

Kinesthetic learners respond to physical closeness and physical rewards. They need a pat on the back rather than an A on a paper. You will notice that these students have larger physical reactions than others, and they often use touch in communication. These students either wiggle and jiggle in their seats or slump down for comfort. The temperature of the room, the softness (or hardness) of the seats, and even the comfort of the clothes they wear are important.

Teaching to the Modalities

It is really not as difficult as some might think to teach to the modalities. Most teachers include at least two in every lesson. We usually have some sort of visual, such as a handout, overhead, or textbook page. Most of us use discussion in every lesson, so that just leaves the kinesthetic component, which many of us forget or feel doesn't fit in. First of all, let's look at the basic fact that we all teach the way we want to learn. Because I am very visual, most of my lessons consist of visual stimuli. I love to read to my students, but my visual students would rather do it themselves (thank you very much!), and I need to offer them the opportunity to at least follow along in the book I am reading. Beware if you are an auditory teacher. The students soon discover your desire to talk and will have you on several different tangents, using valuable class time. Kinesthetic teachers would be much too hands-on for me, but they have a gift that means a great deal to the kinesthetic learner.

Here are some tips for teaching VAK (visual-auditory-kinesthetic):

1. Be sure to include each modality in every lesson.

2. Vary the modality you begin with. Some kinesthetic students will be lost until you get them up and moving—don't always save that for last.

3. Focus time for the brain on a good day is the student's age in minutes. That means seven-year-olds can pay attention for about seven minutes. This is the perfect time to change your strategy from one modality to the next. You can stay on topic; just change the approach.

4. Remember that auditory learners need to talk as much as they need to listen. Provide these opportunities.

5. Kinesthetic learning does not require the student to perform an experiment or "become an adverb." It simply means that these students need to move. Provide movement activities as simple as changing seats, working on team projects, and stretching.

6. Learn to speak the language of the learner. Visual learners often use words such as "I see what you mean" or "I get the picture." Auditory learners might say "I hear what you're saying" or "That sounds good." Kinesthetic learners use phrases such as "That grabs me" or "I can't get a handle on it." Try to key in on these phrases and use them when you speak to the student on an individual basis.

7. After presenting a lesson and assigning some seat work, observe which students need extra help. Perhaps there is a modality you are not giving enough attention to. For example, if most of the students coming up to your desk for help are auditory, you may need to stress the discussion part of the lesson next time.

Many students are great at getting information in all the modalities. So, the majority of your class will be fine with the way you are presently teaching. Those struggling few are the ones who may really benefit from some small changes. You are actually honoring the differences between students by trying to "speak their language." Information makes much more sense to them when it comes to them the way they prefer it. Affording the students the opportunity to discover their own learning modality may help them with homework and testing. This knowledge can go a long way. Figure 6.1 is a learning style inventory that you may want to give to your students. Have them circle each statement they feel applies to them.

The answer key is as follows:

Learning Styles Test Answers

Visual Statements: 1, 4, 6, 9, 12, 19, 30, 34, 35, 37, 39, 40, 43, 44, 45

Auditory Statements: 3, 5, 8, 11, 13, 16, 18, 20, 21, 25, 27, 33, 36, 38, 42

Kinesthetic Statements: 2, 7, 10, 14, 15, 17, 22, 23, 24, 26, 28, 29, 31, 32, 41

Count the number of circled statements in each category. The style with the most circles should be their strongest modality.

THE EIGHT INTELLIGENCES

To deal with the class I described at the beginning of this book and similar situations, I used the theory of multiple intelligences described by Howard Gardner in his 1985 book, *Frames of Mind*. After reading this book, I felt I had permission to try some nontraditional methods of teaching.

Figure 6.1   Learning Style Test

Circle the number of each statement that is true of you.

1. I am aware of what I wear. I like to follow the trends.
2. I like to be comfortable at all times.
3. When the radiator kicks on, I forget what I am doing or saying.
4. I like books with pictures.
5. I prefer to give an oral book report.
6. I like to write long essays.
7. I often lean back in my chair.
8. I don't have to look at people when they talk to me and I still know what they said.
9. When I am angry, I give people dirty looks.
10. When I am angry, I throw things.
11. Sometimes when I'm mad, I mutter under my breath so I don't get in trouble.
12. I hate it when teachers read to me.
13. I like to hear myself read.
14. If a book doesn't have a lot of action in it, I don't like it.
15. I don't want to watch the teacher show us how to do something. I want to try it myself.
16. When the fire drill rings, I shout at people to leave.
17. I usually don't read directions to put things together.
18. I like to mimic others speaking.
19. I like to look you in the eye when you speak.
20. I like to see your mouth when you speak.
21. I like listening to most music.
22. I tap out a beat to the music.
23. Sometimes I learn better when I slouch in my seat.
24. If all the teacher does is lecture, I may as well fall asleep.
25. I can talk for hours about my favorite topics.
26. I like to use the computer to keep my attention.
27. Sometimes I use my voice to scare people.
28. I'm pretty good at sports.
29. I get in trouble sometimes because I can't sit still in class.
30. When the fire drill rings, I look for a place to run.
31. When the fire drill rings, I run out the door before anyone else has a chance.
32. I like a pat on the back to show me that I've done a good job.
33. I like to hear that I've done a good job.
34. I like to read comments about my work.
35. I like an assignment like a poster or a brochure.
36. I like to interview people.
37. If you like me, you'll smile at me or buy me things.
38. If you like me, you'll say nice things to me.
39. If I don't like what you say, I will roll my eyes.
40. On the computer, I like word processing.
41. On the computer, I prefer virtual reality.
42. On the computer, I like musical problem solving.
43. I notice what others are wearing.
44. I like to look at time lines to organize my thoughts.
45. My desk is always neatly arranged.

Prior to the publication of Gardner's work, it was thought that there were only two intelligences: mathematical/logical and verbal/linguistic. Only those two were included on intelligence tests. They were relatively easy to measure and satisfied this country for a long time. Through Project Zero at Harvard, seven intelligences were acknowledged (Gardner, 1985). In 1998, an eighth was added. Through the theory of multiple intelligences, the following are recognized:

Verbal/linguistic

Mathematical/logical

Musical/rhythmic

Visual/spatial

Bodily/kinesthetic

Interpersonal

Intrapersonal

Naturalist

Since 1998, existential intelligence has been added. Someone with a strong existential intelligence is thought to have a sensitivity and capacity to tackle deep questions about existence. This person would look at the big picture as far as the existence of other forms of life in the universe. Since most of us do not tackle religious or philosophical issues in our teaching, this section will focus on the first eight. The eight intelligences are possible ways of expressing one's intelligence. Not all students are high in each area, but we all have potential for every intelligence.

We have potential for every intelligence.

Table 6.2 offers you a quick overview of the characteristics and identifiers of each intelligence.

Verbal/linguistic: The potential to use language. These students think and express themselves with words. They are often good storytellers. This type of intelligence usually fosters a good vocabulary. You might find someone with this intelligence becoming a teacher or a talk show host.

Mathematical/logical: The potential for manipulating numbers and for understanding cause and effect. This intelligent student will be a logical thinker or problem solver. They have a tendency to use numbers easily, ask questions, and be quite precise. Bankers and stockbrokers fall into this category.

Table 6.2   Multiple Intelligence Chart

Intelligence	Characteristics	Identifiers
Verbal/linguistic	Uses language effectively	Tells stories, good vocabulary, enjoys reading, spells well
Mathematical/logical	Has good reasoning and/or number skills	Enjoys mental math, plays strategy games, asks questions
Musical/rhythmic	Discriminates musical forms, is sensitive to sounds	Hums, sings, plays musical instrument, collects music, taps
Visual/spatial	Creates mental images, is aware of objects in space	Easily reads maps and charts, draws well; daydreams
Bodily/kinesthetic	Is skilled in balance, coordination, and movement; expresses through whole body	Is good at competitive sports; moves, fidgets, wiggles; touches others when talking
Interpersonal	Interacts well with others, empathic, handles relationships	Is a team leader, has a large circle of friends, is cooperative
Intrapersonal	Is aware of own feelings, handles own emotions	Is independent, self-confident, self-motivated
Naturalist	Recognizes patterns, classifies—especially flora and fauna	Collects, organizes, and classifies objects; has pets; has green thumb

Musical/rhythmic: The potential for thinking in music and sound. These students are somewhat sound sensitive. They not only enjoy music and rhythm but also are very aware of patterns. Humming, singing, and finding the beat with their fingers or feet are not unusual. These students may become musicians or audiologists, or affiliation with the recording business may be the direction for these students.

Visual/spatial: The potential for representing and manipulating the world in one's mind. You'll want your airline pilot to have this intelligence! These people create mental images and are aware of how objects look and move in space. They may draw, doodle, like puzzles, and work on or create their own mazes. Architects and designers have this intelligence.

Bodily/kinesthetic: The potential for using the whole body or parts for crafting, dancing, and athletics. Here's one for Tiger Woods. This intelligence is exhibited by good motor skills and graceful body movements. Competitive sports are often enjoyed by those with this intelligence. Don't get tunnel vision here. Your surgeon needs to possess this intelligence, as do dancers and athletes!

Interpersonal: The potential for working with others. This is one part of emotional intelligence. This person is sensitive to the feelings of others. He or she also interacts well with people, is good at sharing, and makes a great team member. Therapists, teachers, and talk show hosts are among the many occupations for this intelligence.

Intrapersonal: The potential for understanding oneself and recognizing one's own strengths and weaknesses. This is the other emotional intelligence. These are thinkers and observers. They understand their own emotions. Journaling is often a good activity for these individuals. Writers and philosophers exhibit this intelligence.

Naturalist: The potential for categorizing and classifying the world around us. Another pattern seeker, the naturalist likes animals and plants. The great outdoors is where he or she wants to be and may very well respond better to learning. Classifying and categorizing come easily to this intelligence. The naturalists in my classrooms usually had one or more pets and knew quite a bit about each species. Florists, naturalists, veterinarians, and outdoor recreation directors possess these skills.

Over the years, the question has been asked, "Do we teach *to* the intelligences, or do we teach *with* them?" Most multiple-intelligence schools work on themes or units that enable the intelligences to emerge. Remember that difficult class I was talking about? Here's what I did.

Shakespeare. Does it sound crazy? It worked. I took those kids down to the gymnasium. After finding some shortened versions of *Hamlet* and *Macbeth*, we started talking about who wanted to do what. My two most raucous boys wanted to be stars. (They quickly skimmed the plays and discovered sword fighting!)

Some of the students were interested in props and scenery. Some wanted to come up with music for the scenes. They really became emotionally involved in the whole production. Everyone had to read the plays to understand what was to be done. We discussed the scenes together on the floor in the middle of the gym (except for the two sword fighters, who were off "practicing"). We spent most of every day working on the plays. I combined literature, grammar and punctuation, and English history lessons into the unit. We had to do math to figure light angles and to coordinate movements on stage. Science was spent creating special effects, like the witches' brew at the beginning of *Macbeth*.

It was truly an incredible experience. It took six to eight weeks to get everything done. By then, the students were ready for a performance. We had two, one during the day for the rest of the school and one in the evening for their parents. The students couldn't have been prouder, nor could their teacher.

I use a self-assessment with my students (see Figure 6.2). They enjoy filling in the chart and talking about what they enjoy because they feel good about it. You may want to do the activities in Table 6.3 before they fill out the assessment form. These may give them a feel for each of the intelligences. From these

Figure 6.2   Self-Assessment

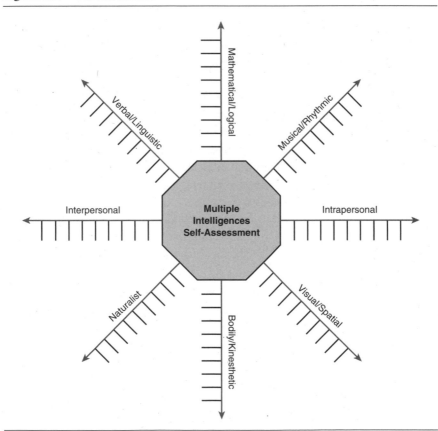

NOTE: Students fill in as many spaces as they think represent their intelligence in each area.

Table 6.3 Intelligence Activities to Help Identify Strengths

Intelligence	Activity	How Are You Smart?
Verbal/linguistic	Ask students to recall a previously memorized poem or portion of text from prior years.	Was this an easy task? Do you enjoy this type of word play?
Mathematical/logical	Give students a mental math problem to solve or one needing pencil and paper.	How did you feel about this task? Do you enjoy playing with numbers?
Musical/rhythmic	Ask students to tap out a rhythm to a song, hum a few bars, or sing.	Did you enjoy this? Or is this something you hesitate to do?
Visual/spatial	Ask students to close their eyes and describe the classroom in detail.	Did you recall such details as the chipping paint? Or the color of the bulletin board?
Bodily/kinesthetic	Describe to your students in detail a physical activity such as riding a horse, being on a runaway train, or some dance moves.	Could you feel the movements? Can you imagine yourself in these situations? Was this a difficult task?
Interpersonal	Ask students to interview each other about a specific idea, such as their most embarrassing moment. Have them construct the questions.	How hard or easy was it to come up with the questions? Do you enjoy talking with people?
Intrapersonal	Ask students to write down their strengths and weaknesses.	How well do you know yourself? Do you need to ask others to determine your strengths?
Naturalist	Ask students to write down answers or discuss the following statements: I have multiple pets. I have a green thumb. I have a collection. I can identify trees by their leaves.	Are any of these true of you? Do you like to categorize or classify objects? How do you feel about being outdoors?

"Can't you give me brains?"
asked the Scarecrow.

"You don't need them. You
are learning something every
day. A baby has brains, but it
doesn't know much.
Experience is the only thing
that brings knowledge. . . ."

assessments, I may form teams with as many different intelligences on them as possible. I find that the students work together better when they are not competing for the same tasks.

From the experience of using the multiple intelligences to teach Shakespeare to that difficult class, I continued my work on brain research, learning, and intelligence. Offering opportunities for students to explore and exhibit known talents, as well as explore and expand new skills and talents, is exciting and rewarding. Using the multiple intelligences is another way to do this.

BRAINS, BLOOM, INTELLIGENCE, AND STYLE

How can we incorporate higher levels of thinking with using learning styles or multiple intelligences? I am hooked on the New Bloom's Taxonomy (Anderson et al., 2001) that I mentioned briefly in Chapter 3 in relation to challenges. The New Bloom is similar to the original Bloom, but it uses all verbs. The original and revised versions are in Table 6.4.

The reason for the revision is clear. Thinking is active; therefore, the words associated with it should also be active words. Incorporated into this taxonomy are both definitions and questions. Table 6.5 shows the key words and ideas associated with each level of the new taxonomy. I have found the importance of this taxonomy in part is its support of the scientifically based strategies for raising student achievement. According to *Classroom Instruction That Works* (Marzano, Pickering, & Pollack, 2001), identifying similarities and differences (comparing, classifying) and summarizing will raise student achievement more than any other strategies. So, how can we incorporate this into the use of learning styles and intelligences? The activity chart (Table 6.6) can help us see how we can combine Bloom with the multiple intelligences.

For the learning styles, we can use the same activities keeping in mind that the visual learner will probably enjoy the same activities as the verbal/linguistic or visual/spatial learner. The auditory learner may like the musical/rhythmic or mathematical/logical ideas. The kinesthetic learner may be more comfortable with the bodily/kinesthetic, visual/spatial, or naturalist views.

Honoring our students' learning styles and intelligences will enable them to have experiences that are meaningful to them. From those experiences, they can gain the knowledge they will need to continue their journey and become lifelong learners.

Table 6.4 Comparison of Bloom's Original Taxonomy and the New Bloom's Taxonomy

Bloom's Original Taxonomy	The New Bloom's Taxonomy
Knowledge	Remember
Comprehension	Understand
Application	Apply
Analysis	Analyze
Synthesis	Create
Evaluation	Evaluate

SOURCE: Anderson et al., 2001

Table 6.5 The New Bloom's Taxonomy

Level of Thinking	Key Words and Ideas
Remember	Recognize information stored in memory, recall information stored in memory
Understand	Interpret, summarize, show examples, classify, infer, compare, explain
Apply	Execute knowledge
Analyze	Differentiate, organize, attribute
Create	Generate, plan, produce
Evaluate	Check, critique

LEARNING PROFILES

By understanding our students' preferred learning style and their multiple intelligences, we can help them use their strengths to learn and remember our curriculum. Offering them options to show us what they know helps relieve their stress and test anxiety. Once they know that they know, we ask them to stretch and use different means of demonstrating the same concepts. As we will see in the next chapter, using multiple systems aids in long-term memory.

Table 6.6 Thinking Activities for the Multiple Intelligences and Each Level of the New Bloom

	Remember	Understand	Apply	Analyze	Create	Evaluate
Verbal/ linguistic	Tell, describe	Summarize, compare, exemplify	Examine, record, classify	Design a questionnaire	Write a play	Debate, create a booklet
Mathematical/ logical	Record, arrange	Compare/contrast, infer	Solve, apply	Interview, measure	Support an idea	Estimate, appraise
Musical/ rhythmic	Sing, repeat	Compare, exemplify	Make up a puzzle game	Arrange, compare	Write a song, poem, rap	Appraise, criticize
Visual/ spatial	Draw, label, illustrate	Illustrate, build, make a cartoon strip	Make a diorama	Make a flow chart	Design a magazine cover	Form a panel, Revise
Bodily/ kinesthetic	Show, tell	Cut out or draw pictures, act out, build	Construct a model	Construct a graph	Invent a machine	Select, perform
Interpersonal	Tell someone, describe	Translate, paraphrase, summarize	Interpret, relate	Inquire, interview	Generate a new product	Recommend, judge, negotiate
Intrapersonal	Write, reflect	Outline, translate	Interpret, solve	Investigate, diagram, reflect	Write about your feelings	Infer, deduce
Naturalist	Label, classify	Classify, locate	Categorize, display, collect photos	Inspect, classify, investigate	Formulate a plan	Verify, categorize

We're Off to See . . .

Since we have explored ways to reach students by their learning profiles, we need to now approach memory and how it works. Can we teach students to have better memories? Do memory preferences influence the way we teach and the way they learn? The next chapter will discuss these questions.

WIZDOM

Key Points to Ponder

1. Your learning style may influence the way you teach.

2. Honoring learning styles can affect brain growth.

3. Multiple intelligences and modalities are options for reaching our students and meeting their needs.

4. Cognitive development is individual; every brain is unique.

Suggestions

- Combining learning style information with multiple intelligence potential offers classroom teachers additional opportunities to reach more students through many and varied strategies.
- There are five sensory modalities, of which we've discussed three at length (visual, auditory, and kinesthetic). Gustatory is taste, and although we have students who love to put things in their mouths, there is usually a stronger modality preference for learning. The olfactory sense, smell, is very powerful for learning and memory. It is difficult to use in the classroom because we have so many sensitive students. You might check for allergies and try bringing in some fragrances.
- Information on learning styles provides a useful framework for understanding learners and identifying gaps in our teaching methods. Check your lesson plans for gaps and redundancies.
- Observation is an excellent determiner of learning styles. A paper-and-pencil inventory may be biased toward certain learners. Hone your observation skills.
- Rather than label students, use the knowledge to determine if your approach to subject matter offers choice and variety.

7 If I Only Had a Memory

Improving Memory to Raise Student Achievement

What would you do with a brain if you had one?

—Dorothy

> The contestants are in their seats. Four players are in the front of the room in pairs. It's time to play *Password!* Our definition of *Password* is simple: If you can play this game and remember the words associated with each idea or concept, you'll probably pass the upcoming test!
>
> I hand one player an index card that has the concepts written on it. One student is the timer. Another is the scorekeeper. The player begins. She gives words associated with what is written on the card, "Setting, plot, characters...." Her partner quickly responds, "Elements of the short story!" They get a point. The play turns to the other contestants. I hand one card and he begins, "An idea, something the author is saying...." His partner immediately responds, "Theme." A point for them.
>
> The entire class is paying attention to what is happening. Many have their hands clasped over their mouths, so they don't blurt out answers. They are awaiting their turn to play the game. This is one review of many yet to come as we tackle genres and what makes them similar and different.

The game keeps the students begging for more. The point is to help get information into long-term memory in a fun and interesting way. Repetition, associations, emotion, and a little competition go a long way in producing good results. This game works for conceptual memory, procedural memory, and factual memory and is great for vocabulary.

> Memory is not merely the only evidence we have of learning; it is also the only evidence we have of self.

I want to share with you the importance of finding the kind of brain the Scarecrow desires. Memory is not merely the only evidence we have of learning; it is also the only evidence we have of *self.* Without our memories, we have no identity. With them, we can be whoever we want to be.

MEMORY DEVELOPMENT

Although it is difficult to pinpoint memory development due to the differences in brain development, there are a few milestones we can consider. According to Jane Healy (2004), by the age of three months, babies have recognition memory for items they are familiar with, such as certain toys and objects they see or experience often. So, they can differentiate between new items and familiar ones. Before their first birthday, most can remember where a toy is hidden, indicating that their working memory is indeed working!

Preschoolers switch from a strong visual memory to a stronger verbal memory as their language skills increase. They actually begin talking to themselves to help with memory. This is a first sign of rehearsal.

Memory strategies begin to be used by age six. They are not very good or effective, but skills like these can be taught. The ability to retell events of a story is quite good at this age. According to Ruby Payne (2005), thinking in stories is something the brain enjoys, and quite often children put information into story form.

As children enter adolescence, their brains make great changes. One of these is an increase in the capacity of working memory. This short-term memory process begins to keep new information in mind as it accesses prior knowledge and makes connections. Sometime during adolescence, working memory should increase to the adult ability to hold up to seven bits of information.

Sense and Significance Affect Memory

"I get it, but I don't like it," Graylin announces as he hands in his paper. I had given my prealgebra students some problems to solve in class. We had only been working with the concepts for a few days, and I didn't think they were ready for homework.

"You got every problem right!" I tell him excitedly as I look over the paper.

"I know. I said I get it. But what am I ever going to use this stuff for?" he asks sincerely. "I'm going to work in my brother's garage. I need to know engines!"

One of the dilemmas we face is that of determining what is relevant and what is simply understood. We have much in our curriculum that is irrelevant to some students and simply makes no sense to others. Consider punctuation. Most students understand its significance when they are reading or are read to. But many students simply don't remember it; it is nonsense to them. The rules make no sense or are unimportant to them, and therefore they don't go into long-term memory. However, a student who is going to write for the school newspaper or who wants to be published finds great significance in punctuation, and the "survival" value of the information is strong enough to make him or her learn the rules.

> One of the dilemmas we face is that of determining what is relevant and what is simply understood.

Graylin understood the work he was doing, but it was insignificant to him. The chances of it going into long-term memory are slimmer than for those who see the significance of it in their lives.

Malcolm Gladwell, author of *The Tipping Point* (2002), refers to the "stickiness factor." What makes things stick so we remember them? He summarizes several studies, two of which are supportive of the sense and significance factors. The first study was with five-year-olds and what they watch on television. Two groups of children were placed into two different rooms to watch a *Sesame Street* show. One group watched an original show, in which the sequencing was appropriate. The other group watched a version of the show in which the key scenes were presented out of order. The first group watched the show and picked up various concepts, while the second simply quit watching. If it didn't make sense, they wouldn't watch.

A second study was done with Yale University students. One group was given a brochure stating the dangers of tetanus in a very dramatic way in order to scare the students into getting inoculated. The other group received a brochure with the same clinical information but without the fear factor. Neither group showed a significant rate of inoculations. However, when the study was repeated, both brochures contained information about the times the school clinic gave the shots. The incidence of inoculations went up

> **Sense plus Significance = Stickiness**

significantly in both groups. The stickiness factor was personalizing the information by allowing students to fit the clinic visit into their schedules. So, once the information became practical (sensible) and personal (significant), it was also sticky (memorable).

If you look at Table 7.1, you can see that something that is significant and sensible will be the most memorable.

Table 7.1 Memory Is Related to Whether Students Understand and Whether It Is Important to Them

Highly memorable	Sense and significance *(I get it and I want to know it.)*
Moderately memorable	Sense and insignificance *(I get it, but I don't need it or want it.)*
Somewhat memorable	Nonsense and significance *(I don't get it, but I want to!)*
Not memorable	Nonsense and insignificance *(I don't get it, and I don't care about it.)*

When Sense Becomes Nonsense!

I have a fabulous lesson plan. I worked hard. My targets are clear and they're up on the board. The students know what I am after. I have a great opening to hook my students. We're beginning the Greek mythology unit that I love.

I start out with, "How many of you like soap operas?" The girls perk up; the boys moan. "How about monsters and wars and gory stuff?" Suddenly the boys are interested. "Aha!" I think to myself. "I've got them!"

I begin the story of creation as it is outlined in mythology. Albeit, I have a shorter and simpler version for these kids, but I follow the story and add my own emotion. They hang on every word.

"Boy, this is going better than I could have hoped for!" I say to myself. "I was going to stop here, but I'm just going to keep going! This is good stuff!"

As I carry on and add new names to the Greek family tree I have on the board, I start to notice some changes in the students. A few are whispering. Some are looking out the window. I see Gabe pull a comic out of his desk.

I realize my mistake. I've gone too far. I blew it!

I had them in the palm of my hand. It was all making sense to them. But I made a critical mistake. I didn't keep track of their focus time. When I planned my lesson, I had decided to stop after 10 or 12 minutes. That's what these seventh graders could handle. But when I thought they were with me and I could continue, I began to lose them. No matter how good it was, their brains only have so much time to focus on one kind of sensory stimulation. I was doing all the talking, and, although they were interested, I passed the point of no return for those brains. The sense I was making became nonsense, the "blah, blah, blah," we see in "Peanuts" cartoons. The part of the brain they were using to take in the information had worn out, and I began wasting time—mine and theirs.

After that crucial point, there would be no memory of what I was sharing.

It's important to remember that if we want higher-level thinking and long-term memories, we have to keep focus time in mind. Table 7.2 shows us what research suggests for focus time (DeFina, 2003). Keep in mind that these times are approximate. On a good day my seventh graders could focus for about 12 minutes. I tried to keep each teaching session to about 10 minutes to be safe.

Table 7.2   Focus Time for Each Grade Level

Age	Focus Time
Kindergarten	4–6 minutes
First grade	5–7 minutes
Second grade	6–8 minutes
Third grade	7–9 minutes
Fourth grade	8–10 minutes
Fifth grade	9–11 minutes
Sixth grade	10–12 minutes
Seventh grade	11–13 minutes
Eighth grade	12–14 minutes
Ninth grade	13–15 minutes
Tenth grade	14–16 minutes
Eleventh grade	15–17 minutes
Twelfth grade	16–18 minutes

NOTE: These times are not absolute, as brains develop differently. These are the times that students can focus on a good day. Stress, sleepiness, and other factors can affect these times.

MEMORY PRINCIPLES

> "Please stand up!" Mr. Stern asks his class. "Find a partner. With your partner take turns sharing the ideas that you learned today."
>
> Angie turns to Taunya, "Well, first of all, food and oxygen go through the cell membrane."
>
> Taunya looks surprised. "I thought this lesson was about changes in our bodies."
>
> "It's about cell division," Angie replies.
>
> "But what about the fact that we're taller?" Taunya asks.
>
> "Why don't you tell me what ideas you think we were supposed to get from this lesson?" Angie asks.
>
> "I don't know. I thought we were going to talk about mitosis. So, I kept waiting for Mr. Stern to say that word and then I was going to write things down. But when he asked about our hair growing and our nails, I figured he was changing the plan."

Mr. Stern learns a lot about what students are remembering from these frequent conversations. Students will remember what they deem important—

Clear targets provide necessary information to help "frame" the learning.

and what makes sense, as I said earlier. But we also need to look back at Chapter 2. Do Mr. Stern's students have a clear target? If we want memory to be successful, the brain needs to know what it must remember. Clear targets provide necessary information to help frame the learning. From there, feedback continues to frame and reframe what the brain is storing.

Dr. Fiona McPherson (2004) describes three basic principles of how memory works. First, there is the *code principle:* Memories are selected and maneuvered as representations of memory. In other words, memories are not reproduced per se; they are redesigned. Then she writes about the *network principle:* The codes are linked together through associations. Then, through the *domino principle,* a code is activated, which in turn activates another code. Information is remembered based on what each individual selects to code and what each individual emphasizes.

Retrieving a memory is tricky if you don't know where to look. Your brain may store information, but without the organization that you can offer, you may not know where it is stored. The more systems we use to store information, the easier it is to find.

EXPLICIT AND IMPLICIT MEMORY

Memory is divided into two categories. Explicit memory is sometimes called declarative memory because we can "declare" it, that is, talk about it. There are two memory systems that fall under this category: **semantic memory** and

episodic memory. Semantic memory is our memory for facts and concepts. Episodic memory is for locations and events. These can be tied together under the network principle. For instance, I love animals. All of my life I have had at least one dog, so I have a lot of dog information stored in my brain. Some of the information I can tie directly to specific episodes, whereas other bits of information are more semantic in nature—trivial information I have picked up throughout my life. Perhaps some of this occurred through events, but I can no longer remember the events. This network might look like Figure 7.1. It contains episodic memories, like my dog Trixie dying when I was a little girl, and semantic memories, like the facts that dogs bark and shed.

Implicit memory consists of nondeclarative memories. These are memories that we don't consciously bring to mind. They are either **emotional memories, procedural memories,** or **conditioned response (automatic) memories.** We don't think about each movement we make when we ride a bike; we just ride. We don't try to form emotional memories; they just form. And conditioned responses, like saying "Gesundheit" when someone sneezes, are habit. Table 7.3 shows the five memory systems.

Figure 7.1   Part of My Memory Network for "Dog"

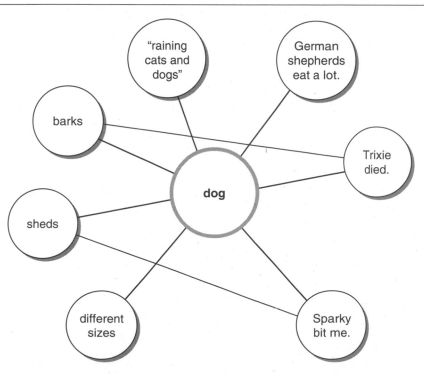

Table 7.3   Categories and Systems of Memory

Category	System	Description	Example
Explicit	1. Semantic	Words, facts, textbook material	The presidents, states, and their capitals
Explicit	2. Episodic	Locations, events	Remembering information that was written on the board and is no longer there
Implicit	3. Procedural	Muscle memory, movements that have been repeated	Riding a bike, driving a car
Implicit	4. Emotional	Related to strong emotional experiences	A personal story, something that scared you
Implicit	5. Conditioned response	Habits that have been formed through conditioning	I say "hot"; you say "cold"

From Sensory Memory to Long-Term Memory

I want to include at this point the seven steps I have developed to help teachers take students from receiving sensory information to forming long-term retrievable memories (Sprenger, 2005). In the past, I always followed the format for forming memories in the conventional way as shown in Figure 7.2. But in truly understanding the progression of memory from sensory to long-term, the chart would look more like that in Figure 7.3.

Step One: Reach and Teach

This step consists of getting students' attention and motivating them to learn. We must get students to attend to incoming sensory information. The most powerful way to do this is through emotion. We can also use novelty, interaction, technology, and other hooks.

Figure 7.2 Typical Progression of Information From Sensory to Long-Term Memory (From Differentiation Through Learning Styles and Memory)

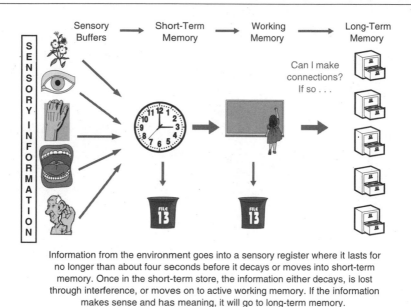

Information from the environment goes into a sensory register where it lasts for no longer than about four seconds before it decays or moves into short-term memory. Once in the short-term store, the information either decays, is lost through interference, or moves on to active working memory. If the information makes sense and has meaning, it will go to long-term memory.

Step Two: Reflect

Reflection is an underused strategy. It appears to be fluff because of the time it takes. I tell teachers that reflection is the first rehearsal. The students need the opportunity to think of what the new learning is and connect it to prior learning. This involves some time. It can be done through journaling, talking with a partner, drawing, or visualizing. This is necessary to take the information from sensory memory to immediate memory. It is here where the memory process lasts only seconds unless it is worked with and goes to working memory. I have previously referred to working memory in relation to the prefrontal cortex. Again, this is a process by which the brain takes the old and the new information, checks to see if it fits together, and decides it is worth saving for the long term or simply throws it away. Working memory is an important process and is vital to learning and comprehension.

Step Three: Recode

In this step, students take information and put it into their own words. Research supports this practice as imperative for long-term understanding.

Figure 7.3   Memory: Step-by-Step

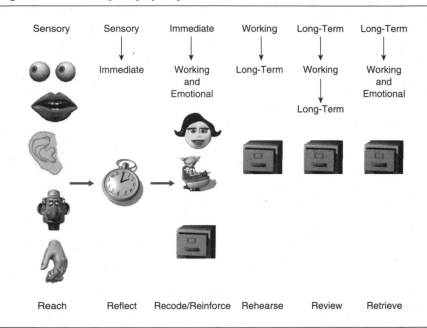

So, from the reflective step, they begin the working memory process by doing some form of personalization. This may be done through the scientifically based practices of identifying similarities and differences, summarizing, or paraphrasing. If they truly understand, they can put it into words. For various learning styles, drawing, acting, and speaking are also acceptable.

Step Four: Reinforce

This is time for feedback. Students now need to know whether their recoding efforts paid off. They are still working with the information in working memory, and feedback helps them to frame the learning. It is time that they discover whether their understandings are correct. Reinforcement is a step that should take place throughout a lesson or a unit. This is the turning point for long-term memory. We don't want incorrect information to be permanently stored.

> **Reinforcement is a crucial step in the memory process.**

Step Five: Rehearse

This is the time to start using the new information with the five memory systems, multiple intelligences, and learning styles. The more areas of the brain we use to store the information, the more retrievable it will be. Rehearsal takes information from working memory and begins to place it in long-term memory.

Step Six: Review

The review process should be done throughout the unit. Then it should be continued through the school year. If the material is going to be questioned on a standardized assessment, review is crucial. Review also gives students some feedback. It is possible along the way of doing homework and practice that their conceptions went astray. Review will help them focus on the learning that they may be having difficulty with. Review allows them to take information that has been stored in long-term memory, retrieve it, manipulate it, and then store it again in various formats.

Step Seven: Retrieve

Information will be retrievable if the previous steps have been followed. Utilizing the episodic system by testing in the same room that the material was given may make a difference to some students in how much information is retrieved. Test preparation will be helpful along with addressing any test anxiety the students may have.

MEMORY LANES = MEMORY SYSTEMS

The five memory systems shown in Table 7.3 have been suggested by current research as the roads to success for our students. I can travel up and down Sheridan Road all day, but if you live on Main Street, I will never find you. So it is with memory. There are special systems for specific types of memory. We need to know how to store memories in each system and how to retrieve memories from them. Each system is associated with a brain structure, but keep in mind that it takes many networks in different parts of the brain to store and activate memories for any of the systems.

It takes many networks in different parts of the brain to store and activate memories.

Semantic Memory

This is the memory system for words. Facts, concepts, ideas, and lists we get from books, lectures, and videos are stored here. The semantic system is associated with the hippocampus. Important information in the form of facts must be consolidated through the hippocampus if it is to be held in long-term memory. Semantic information is the most difficult information to remember and retrieve. To be really successful at doing so could make you a champion at "Trivial Pursuit." The difficulty lies in the fact that the information has to go to working memory first. Working memory is a process in which information is held in the prefrontal cortex. Here, it is rehearsed, elaborated on, and worked with until it can be stored in long-term memory.

This information must be processed often for it to stick. This would mean discussing a few paragraphs of text material at a time. It could also mean outlining, mind mapping, role-playing—and repetition, repetition, repetition. Because remembering semantic information is sometimes difficult, many people have created books full of semantic tricks. There are such mnemonic devices as acrostics, acronyms, peg systems, word pictures, and location systems. See Table 7.4 for a list of common mnemonics for different subjects. The best way to remember text information is to put it into another memory system. As teachers, we do this all the time; however, we are not always cognizant of our strategies. For instance, I have been fortunate to become involved with an English grammar and writing curriculum called the Shurley Method (information accessible at http://www.shurleyenglish.com). After teaching grammar for 12 years, I finally found material that worked, and there are reasons for its success. One reason is that the method uses many of the other memory systems for storage. It provides jingles, rhythm, and a flow that promotes fast and easy learning. These strategies access memory systems that make learning grammar easy.

It is important to follow the seven-step method when dealing with semantic information. Since this type of information requires the short-term memory processes of immediate and working memory, following the steps allows you to methodically get this information into long-term memory. This system is the paper-and-pencil system that is used on standardized tests. The steps guide you toward putting the information in multiple systems and practicing with the semantic system for summative assessments.

Episodic Memory

The hippocampus also consolidates episodic memory. This is a kind of factual memory that deals with location and events. In other words, when you learn something, you are in a specific location, and that location can trigger the memory. People often ask, "Where were you when . . . JFK was assassinated? . . . Princess Diana was killed? . . . O. J. Simpson was chased? . . . on 9/11?" Many of us (who are old enough) can associate a location with the details of the event.

Many studies have been performed that prove that people who learn information in a specific location will remember that information better in the same location.

Table 7.4　　Common Mnemonics

Mnemonic	Explanation
Please excuse my dear Aunt Sally.	Parentheses, exponents, multiplication, division, addition, subtraction
Every good boy does fine.	Notes on the treble clef
Lucky cows drink milk.	Roman numerals LCDM (ascending order)
A rat in the house might eat the ice cream.	First letter of each spells arithmetic
Kittens prefer cream or fish, generally speaking.	Kingdom, phylum, class, order, family, genus, species
Divorced, beheaded, died, divorced, beheaded, survived	Six wives of Henry VIII
General Eisenhower's oldest girl rode a pony home yesterday.	First letter of each spells geography
A friend is always there when the *end* comes.	To help spell *friend* correctly
Your principal is your pal.	Distinguish between *principal* and *principle*

The family is preparing for a short vacation. I have just returned from work to finish packing and load the car. My mental list is flashing quickly through my mind: Put food in the cat's dish, mail the house payment, turn on the lights in the living room, and call my sister-in-law to remind her to bring in the mail. Everything except the phone call has been done. I leave my bedroom and head for the office to make the call. As I reach the door to the office, I pause and try to remember why I am there. What was it that I had intended to do? I turn around and go back to the bedroom. There, I remember that I had been going over the list. I repeat the list. The lightbulb goes on: I have to make that call. I hurry back to the office, grab the phone, and begin dialing.

Episodic memory saved me from that old feeling of craziness that happens when these *episodes* occur. The importance of this memory system must not be ignored. Our students value this important opportunity to use memory triggers.

This memory system is activated invisibly. That is to say, students picture information in places where it used to be. Staring at the blank chalkboard or white board is one example. If information had been written there, they may recreate the visual representation in their minds and gather the material. Teachers are also covered with invisible informa-

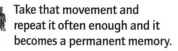
This memory system is activated invisibly.

tion. I was asked to speak to the language arts teachers at a school a few years ago. For the first time, their students had received low writing scores on the state test, and the principal wanted me to help them with their writing strategies. I asked to see some of the writing samples from the test, so the principal contacted the testing company, which sent the school's essays to him.

All I had to do was look at the essays to see what the problem was. The students obviously had not taken the writing test in the language arts classrooms with their writing teachers. I spotted this right away, because the students had written such short essays. Their writing was insufficient, and the state rubrics require a certain length in order to assess the criteria. Sure enough, they had been tested in many different classrooms, including their math, social studies, and science rooms. In these classes, the students were normally expected to write only short-answer essays. When the language arts teachers looked at the tests, they were outraged that their students would write so little. They always expected multiple paragraph essays. Had the students been in the writing classroom and/or with their writing teachers, their memories would have been triggered to write an appropriate response to the writing prompt. Location, location, location!

Creating different atmospheres in your classroom can enhance the episodic memory system. Change bulletin boards for each unit. Use a different seating chart as well. Looking at the world from a new perspective helps make the information fresh and new. Wearing costumes and hats also helps. Although episodic details fade over time, they are excellent triggers for semantic memory information.

Procedural Memory

The procedural memory system is associated with the cerebellum. It is sometimes called muscle memory or bodily-kinesthetic memory. Driving a car and riding a bicycle are two good examples of proce-

Take that movement and repeat it often enough and it becomes a permanent memory.

dural memories. How powerful is this system? Think about it—we never forget those procedures. So, how can we use this system in the classroom?

Providing movement has become a brain-compatible teaching basic. We know from experts Hannaford (2005) and the Dennisons (1994) that movement enhances learning and memory and also strengthens neural connections. Every lesson should contain movement. Take that movement and repeat it often enough, and it becomes a permanent memory. Along with that movement, the learning associated with it also becomes permanent.

In the case of brain damage or brain insults, it can become quite difficult to use and rely on semantic and working memory. For this reason, many individuals who have had brain injuries are taught to surround themselves with procedures to follow. These become natural to the body and enable tasks to be completed quickly and easily without stress.

Role-play, skits, and other productions are avenues to procedural memory. As students involve their bodies in the understanding of concepts and ideas, they form a new understanding of the material.

Keyboarding is a procedural memory after it has been learned completely. Asking a student to create work on the computer can be very difficult, because the brain struggles between trying to be creative and trying to find the keys. It is very important to have students create with paper and pencil until they become so proficient on the keyboard that the struggle is gone.

Automatic/Conditioned Response Memory

Associated with the cerebellum and a midbrain structure called the neostriatum, conditioned response memory is very powerful. It has been called conditioned response memory because the automaticity is a result of conditioning. For instance, the information you have in this system includes antonyms (I say "Stop"; you say "Go."). Multiplication tables, the alphabet, and decoding skills are also stored here. When you are reading a book and, at the end of the page, find yourself without a clue about the content, it is because you were using your decoding skills on the material but you were not using your working memory for comprehension. Perhaps you were thinking about what you were going to do later.

There are many ways to put information into this system. Flash cards put information into conditioned response memory. Rhyme and rhythm are also great ways to do this. I have always used music to help my students remember difficult information. They choose a melody and sing the information. The military "count off" song worked very well for helping verbs. The students would march around the room and sing the words. This added a procedural memory to the learning as well.

Emotional Memory

This memory system begins with the amygdala, the limbic structure that sifts through all incoming information for emotional content. The amygdala is very powerful and can take control of the brain. For this reason, attaching emotional memories to learning can make a tremendous difference in how material is remembered.

I am a strong proponent of storytelling because of its emotional implications. Antonio Damasio (1999), one of the leading neuroscientists in the world, believes in the strength and the natural aptitude we have for stories. Think of a time when a friend or loved one shared an experience with you that was very important to her or him. It may have been a time when this person was wronged in some way. After listening to the story, you may have felt like getting even with the person who wronged your friend. Your friend's strong feelings affected you emotionally, and that is why you remember the story. Emotions are contagious, and if we use this in the classroom, it will help students remember.

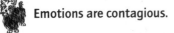
Emotions are contagious.

Surprise is one component of what is called *flashbulb memory.* This is the memory of intensely emotional events. For instance, the question "Where were you when JFK was assassinated?" may bring up a picture in your mind that is nearly photographic. This type of memory, although not accurate over time, is very strong. It activates two memory systems: emotional memory, due to the element of surprise; and episodic memory, because it takes you to a place. If we could make every learning experience for our students as memorable as some of our flashbulb memories, imagine the knowledge they would have!

Alternate Routes

I became a much better teacher when I began to consider the memory systems for each unit I taught. It became a challenge to create some ideas for each system, and it also was fun. The students became involved as well. By suggesting that constructing these memory makers would help them remember, the process worked even better.

Let's look at math. Story problems have always been a mystery to some children, and I was one of those children. All five memory systems can help solve the problem.

Semantic: Here are the rules.

Episodic: Think back to other times and places where you have solved problems.

Procedural: The steps to solving problems are stored here.

Conditioned response: Basic math facts are in this system.

Emotional: Good or bad, success or failure—these are stored here.

The more we practice accessing all five memory systems, the easier it will become. As our students become successful, we will see the fruits of our labor. I have included the model that I use as a guide when planning my teaching units (see Table 7.5).

Table 7.5   Memory System Model: Making the Most of Your Material and Their Memories

Semantic Textbook information, word by word	• What mnemonic devices will be necessary for my students to understand this information? • Which semantic strategies will be used? • Will I need practice tests? • How can I access other systems?	
Episodic Location/events	• How will I decorate my room? • Are there any accessories I can use? • What can I do to make my lesson more like an event? • Are field trips possible? • Where? • When?	
Procedural Muscle memory/ movement	• What can my students "do" to enhance memory? • In what ways can I get my students moving during this unit?	
Conditioned response Automatic	• Will flash cards aid in remembering this material? • Is there information that can be put to music to enhance automatic memory?	
Emotional Priority: feelings and interests	• How will I introduce the unit to access emotions? • Is there any way I can put this information into story form? • How will this information influence my students' lives? • How do I feel about this information, and can I share these feelings?	

NOTE: This model may be used to plan thematic units using the five memory systems. The third column is left blank, so teachers can copy this plan and use it for their lessons.

METACOGNITION

I divide the students into five teams. Each is given one of the memory systems, so that I have semantic, emotional, episodic, procedural, conditioned response teams. We are ready to do some problem-based learning. The question is, "Should drivers be allowed to use cell phones?" The students are excited about this topic and have some of their own stories to tell.

"My mom talks on the phone and puts on makeup when she drives me to school!" shouts one of the boys. "It's a wonder that I'm still alive. She scares me to death."

I tell the semantic team to look for facts. Any statistics on accidents, deaths, number of cell phones in use, and so forth. They begin to brainstorm. The emotional team is already gathering stories. One of the girls shares this information: "Some lady was on 'Oprah' the other day. Her daughter was killed because some guy looked down for a second to dial!" The episodic team is charged with creating the atmosphere: bringing in pictures, posters, and news articles. They are also challenged to write their own story. The procedural team's job is to check out any procedures, rules, or principles already employed relating to cell phone usage. They must also devise rules and techniques that meet their own safety requirements. The conditioned response team is to plan a march on Washington. They must gather evidence for both sides of the issue, plan campaigns, and prepare slogans, songs, and chants.

The room is buzzing as the children discuss, research, and plan. Some are busy on the Internet. Others are heading for the library to search current magazines and books.

The beauty of using the memory systems for this learning, or any learning, is what the students discover about themselves. First, they must use higher-level thinking to gather and create memories for themselves and others. To find an access for any system, the students first have to grasp the information. They must evaluate what parts of the information are valuable and worth remembering.

Students quickly discover which system works best for them.

Then, they must synthesize it to create the memory. This type of problem solving gives students the practice they need to develop complex cognitive skills. Students quickly discover which system works best for them. Thinking about thinking leads them to an understanding of how their minds work for information gathering, encoding, and retrieval.

STEP BY STEP; SYSTEM BY SYSTEM

Let's take a look at how to incorporate the steps and the memory systems by designing a lesson plan. We must start with a clear target.

Targets: Understand what an adverb is. Recognize and label adverbs. Write complete sentences using adverbs.

Assessment: Write a paragraph using adverbs correctly and labeling them.

Reach and Teach: Dress as the "Adverb Lady." Wear words written on masking tape and taped all over your body. Peel a word off and have students make sentences using the word (emotional, procedural).

Reflect: Have students form pairs to talk about an exciting experience and write adverbs to describe it (accessing prior knowledge, emotional).

Recode: Ask students to write a sentence and label adverbs or draw a picture and discuss which words describe what is happening; they should also create a definition of adverbs (semantic).

Reinforce: Cruise the room and read sentences. Ask students to rearrange their sentences and see if they can still label the adverbs (emotional, working memory, semantic).

Rehearse: Have students

Cut sentence strips into individual words and have groups put sentences back together correctly (procedural, emotional).

Go to dictionary.com and look up a definition of *adverb.* Then use the thesaurus there and type in different adverbs. Discuss the synonyms (semantic, procedural).

Find the adverbs in a list of words you give them (semantic).

Do homework in which they must identify and label adverbs in sentences (semantic, episodic).

Create an adverb song defining the word and giving at least 10 examples (conditioned response, emotional).

Create a word wall of adverbs (episodic).

Review:

> Use a koosh ball to toss to a child. The student must say an adverb and then toss the ball to a fellow student with the same directive (procedural, conditioned response).

> Begin a sentence and have students offer adverbs that will be appropriate (semantic).

> Have students write paragraphs together and underline adverbs (semantic, emotional).

This may be a lesson plan that takes several days. Each day you would want to begin with a *reach* step as you again get the students to focus on the information. Many teachers use this first step as a preview and, no matter what step they stop at, they finish with a quick review. This offers another rehearsal for the students before they leave the topic and move on to something else.

The primacy-recency effect is supported by this practice. We remember beginnings and endings better than we remember middles. Short reviews at the end of each lesson support this memory concept.

KANSAS IS RIGHT DOWN MEMORY LANE

Raising student achievement is a priority in our high-stakes educational world. Increasing memory can raise student achievement. By giving students information about how their brains and memories work, they can put more effort into remembering. Clearly, we need to be sure that what we teach makes sense and has significance. Once we have accomplished that, we can focus on the systems that work best for each student.

We're Off to See . . .

All of the information so far has helped in our understanding of the brain and of how to get information from lower levels in the brain to higher levels. Learning how to handle stress, emotion, and learning styles and developing an understanding of memory all lead to more powerful learning experiences for our students. Next, we'll take a look at classroom management by understanding brain states, the impact that music has on the brain, and how movement improves learning.

WIZDOM

Key Points to Ponder

1. Memory is stored in many parts of the brain.

2. There are different memory systems in the brain.

3. Long-term memories are stored in a step-by-step process.

Suggestions

- Mnemonic devices can be used to help students remember more than words or phrases. Acronyms, acrostics, and peg systems can be used to memorize key words that will trigger other memories. For instance, if I have a cue for the Battle of Gettysburg, the name of the battle alone may open up a network of information in my brain and allow me to share a lot of information that I know. Conditioned response memory strategies such as songs work in the same way.

- Can you name the memory systems? Using a simple acronym, we can say that memory c.r.e.e.p.s. in (conditioned response, episodic, emotional, procedural, semantic).

- Ask your students how they are going to study for a specific exam. Have them share their strategies with each other, and offer them a few of your own.

- Some research suggests that working memory can be increased (Klingberg, Forssberg, & Westerberg, 2002). One result of this increase has been higher IQ scores. Help your students increase their working memory by giving them mental problems to solve. This makes them hold information in working memory and add what they already know to solve the problem.

8 The Wicked Witch: What Is She So Upset About?

Calming and Controlling the Classroom

Come with me; and see that you mind everything I tell you, for if you do not, I will make an end of you. . . .

—The Wicked Witch

Blair approaches my desk after I finally found a moment to sit down. Sitting is something I have to remind myself to do. Today, it is easy to sit—I am in one of those moods. I don't want to speak to anyone. As Blair gets closer, she begins to ask a question.

"Don't even think about it!" I snap, in a tone of voice that means trouble.

The bell suddenly rings, and I dismiss the seventh graders. I go to the door to greet the next class, but my heart isn't in it.

"What's the matter?" the kind librarian inquires.

"I don't want to talk about it." The words come out of my mouth quickly and decisively.

Another teacher walks by and asks, "Are you going to the concert tonight?"

"I don't care if I ever go to a concert again! This place is driving me crazy!" With that, I turn around and stomp back into the room. Sorry kids, no greeting at the door today. I've had it!

I sit down again at my desk and pick up my pen. It is shaped in the form of a witch. A gift from a colleague who had visited a Warner Studio store, it fit my mood perfectly. Yes, here I am, the Wicked Witch. But why?

From that time on, I would often let my students (as well as my own children) know that I was in a bad mood by saying, "The Wicked Witch of the West is here today." They knew that it probably wasn't a good time to approach me with any suggestions. What I didn't know was that my bad mood was actually a result of stress. Until I studied brain research, I had no idea how much stress influenced my behavior and how much my behavior affected my classroom.

If stress caused the behavior of the Cowardly Lion, how could stress also have caused the wicked behavior of the witch? The amount of stress we are able to handle varies with circumstances and with the way our unique brains function. In Chapter 4, I discussed the stress response and how to de-stress students. What about teachers?

Just as the students can carry an allostatic load, so can we teachers. We are sometimes not good at handling our own stress. Okay, so I am the Wicked Witch. So what? I can easily calm myself down. Maybe I just need to get away for awhile. That's it! I'll go visit Josh (my son) in Chicago this weekend. I won't take anything with me that even resembles education. No papers. No grade book. No plan book. It'll be great, and I'll return refreshed!

Easier said than done, right? I did go away without any of those items. I ate at nice restaurants. I shopped. Josh and I went to a play. I felt much better. Sunday evening when I got home, I was actually proud of myself for taking care of *me* for a change. And Monday morning . . .

I stand at the door to greet my students. The sun is shining, and I am feeling great. The students enter the room. I walk over to the boom box to turn off the music. As I turn around to speak to the teams, Jay pushes Kent out of his seat. My metamorphosis occurs instantaneously. The Wicked Witch reveals herself again. "What do you think you're doing?" I shout, as though the entire city of Peoria needs to hear this. My tirade continues for several minutes as I lose control. When I finally feel I have gotten enough off my chest and have properly punished Jay (for that was what I was after—punishment, not discipline), I look around at my class. They are stunned. They are quiet and sitting up very straight. I have terrified them.

> **I never use threat in the classroom unless I am under stress . . . unless I feel threatened.**

Power and control. Sometimes, they're just illusions. Other times, we get a little power and abuse it, as was the case that day. What had I done to my students? I was looking out at a classroom of 27 Cowardly Lions, and I had created them. How? That's easy: threat. I *never* use threat in the classroom . . . unless I am under stress . . . unless I feel *threatened*. Why was I feeling threatened?

I had just returned from a relaxing weekend. Why wasn't I handling this situation better? If we compare stress levels to a staircase, with the bottom step being a stress-free condition and the top step being very stressful, we can see what my weekend did for me. On Friday, when I left school, I was on the top step. I had just about had it. I was unwilling to talk to my students or my colleagues. The weekend was great, but had I managed to get back to Step 1? Actually, in that short period of time, it would have been very difficult. I probably returned on Monday to school on about Step 5. It felt so much better than the top step had; I thought I was in excellent emotional condition. The moment a stressor revealed itself, I took a giant leap right up to the top. I needed to figure out how to get to the bottom step—and try to stay there.

Brain research tells us that in a classroom or business situation, hierarchies develop. It's a natural phenomenon. People form groups, and some wind up on the top of the heap, whereas others find themselves stuck at the bottom. The individuals at the top have power. They like to keep it that way. Those at the bottom are experiencing the most stress (Sylwester, 2000). When my life and my classroom were running well, my stress levels were low.

> **Brain research tells us that in a classroom or business situation, hierarchies develop.**

When things got out of hand, I became the most stressed individual in the room. To get that power back, I had to put stress elsewhere. In this case, I stressed the entire class. The question I had to ask myself was "How do I end this cycle?"

MY THEORY OF NEGATIVE REPLACEMENT

I started by looking at my class. What did the hierarchy look like? It was easy to see that Jay was on the bottom. He was always in trouble. What were his stressors? Jay was behind. He had become the class clown in recent months. Did this cover up his lack of academic success? No, it really just disrupted the classroom and took us off task. *On task* was a problem for Jay. If I could get Jay on track, perhaps he would feel less stress and be less impulsive, and my stress levels would go down.

Through the brain research I had been reading, I realized that if I could *fix* Jay, someone else would then be at the bottom of the heap, and that brain would need to do something to affect my hierarchy. For years, I have called this the *theory of negative replacement:* the phenomenon of the most difficult student moving to another school only to be replaced by another problem student. Brain research backs that up. How does one keep the situation from occurring? How could I make the classroom less stressful for the kids and for myself? I had to emphasize the fact that I needed to take care of myself in order to take care of my students. What strategies would make my classroom run more smoothly?

What tools would the brain research support that would also support me in my classroom? Could I really get rid of the Wicked Witch?

EMOTIONS, ATTENTION, AND LEARNING

Emotions are the source of attention. Without attention, there is no learning (Sylwester, 2000). By dealing with the Tin Man in Chapter 5, I knew that I was working on emotional intelligence. But I also had to look at other strategies to keep my classroom managed and my students attending.

I first chose to look at focus time. As I described in the previous chapter, brains have limits. There are differing points of view on which focus strategy to use. Some use the *10, 3, 7* system. For the first focus, 10 minutes are available; then comes a 3-minute diffusion time and a second focus of 7 minutes (Benesh, 1999). When I taught in the primary grades, I found that 10 minutes was just too long for many students. Dr. David Sousa (2006) refers to the *primacy-recency effect.* He believes that 20-minute lessons with downtime are the most efficient. In a 20-minute learning experience, there is about a 13-minute prime time for learning, 2 minutes of down time, and a second prime time for about 5 minutes. When trying this strategy, I found that even with my middle school students, 13 minutes passed a point of no return for some. Although these strategies work for many teachers, I have always relied on age in minutes. On a good day, a 10-year-old has about 10 minutes of focusing availability. So, after about 8 or 10 minutes, it is time to do something different. Students need processing time, which gives them an opportunity to act on their learning (Sprenger, 2005).

I knew I needed to make myself more aware of my time management. It seemed obvious that this particular group of students varied a great deal in development. There were differing emotional levels as well as different focus times. I was not handling my audience well. I was not observing carefully what *states* they were in. Another focus was to look at using music more effectively to handle emotions. By making some adjustments in the classroom in these areas, perhaps I would be able to more productively engage my students' emotions, help them attend to learning, and keep the Wicked Witch at bay.

BRAIN STATES

At any given moment in time, each of us is experiencing a state of mind. We might think of them as moods, but they are really more temporary than that.

These states affect what information we may acquire, because they affect what we are attending to. The brain is constantly learning and trying to make sense of input. It must go through several different states to acquire information. A process called the *learning loop* explains these learning states.

Keep in mind that states are simply moments in time. At these moments, a combination of our physiology, our feelings, the pictures in our minds, and the sounds around us determines our behavior. For example, sit up straight and look at the ceiling. Put a big smile on your face. In this position, with that smile, it is probably very difficult to be "depressed." Sit more slumped in your chair, look down at the floor, breathe slowly, and frown. In this position, it is more difficult to be in the state

> The brain is constantly learning and trying to make sense of input. It must go through several different states to acquire information.

we call "happy." It is easy to change either of these states. Move. That's it. Change that physiology. Look up instead of down. Stand up. Move around. Every movement affects brain chemistry and can affect the state that you are in. Movement changes the body and the brain. It will increase respiration and heart rate as well as change the pattern of brain waves. Neurotransmitters and hormones will be released through movement that will enhance learning (Jensen, 2000c).

Inside Out or Outside In?

It appears that our states come from the inside. Our physiology changes the pictures in our minds. However, research shows that we can also change those states from the outside in! Being in a room with someone in a happy mood, when you are in a sad one, can change the way you feel (Gladwell, 2002). We are even willing to pay for a state change! Have you ever gone to a sad or scary movie? Ridden the highest possible roller-coaster? Listened to a song you knew would make you cry? Headed for the refrigerator when you were tired, stressed, or exhilarated but not truly hungry? We have all done these things without knowing why. We simply needed to change our state. There are times when we need to change the way we are feeling or looking at things. These are states. From a biological point of view, what we are doing is changing the balance of neurotransmitters in our brains.

> When it comes to learning and memory, we need to be aware of positive learning states.

When it comes to learning and memory, we need to be aware of positive learning states. Students need motivation to learn. An important way to motivate them is to appeal to their preferred modalities or learning styles. All states are dependent on modalities. A visual person needs visual stimulation; an auditory person prefers sounds. The kinesthetic learner requires movement or touch.

For the learning loop to work, material must be presented in different modalities. If the presentation is successful, the student first acquires the information and then receives some kind of reinforcement from the teacher. This reinforcement is also modality dependent. An auditory learner needs to hear that he or she did a good job. The visual learner would appreciate a smile or the grade on a paper. The kinesthetic learner needs a handshake or a pat on the back. From these appropriate reinforcements, the learner convinces himself or herself that he or she knows.

States to Avoid

What happens to the student who falls out of the loop, the way my student Jay did? The state the learner falls into first is usually frustration. In the last chapter, we talked about sense and significance. This state occurs when the student cannot make sense of what is being taught. I call it the "I don't get it" state. The visual learners will cock their heads, scrunch up their eyes, and look puzzled. The auditory learners may mumble to themselves, start talking to those around them, and perhaps shake their heads. The kinesthetic learners will start moving and looking for something to do. As a kinesthetic learner, Jay usually did something physical.

At this point, whenever you find your students going off task, it is time to evaluate the lesson and make some changes in the way you are presenting the material. For instance, if you notice that the majority of the students off task have puzzled looks, you may not be teaching with enough visual input. It is crucial to remotivate these students.

If you cannot get the student to a positive learning state, he or she then goes from this state to the state of fear. I call this one the "I'm afraid I'm never going to get it" state. In a fear state, the learner is experiencing stress hormones in the brain and body that can interfere with further learning.

It is usually necessary to provide some movement to *change the student's mind.* In the case of single students, I may send them out of the classroom on an errand or for a drink of water. When they return, they may be better able to focus. Asking another student to help may also change the fear state. Perhaps this is the time for some peer teaching or teamwork.

The universal state of fear affects many of us in similar ways. The visual learner, who usually has great eye contact, suddenly looks down. The auditory learner may start talking more but generally will be very quiet, with eyes moving from side to side. The kinesthetic learner may look down and slouch or try to physically hide. One thing is clear: They are all trying to conceal their lack of understanding, and no one is learning.

If the fear is not dealt with, students may become angry or apathetic. There can be outbursts or simply no response. These are difficult states and require one-on-one attention. They may also require counseling. These are the states in which I usually find Jay.

> **If the fear is not dealt with, students may become angry or apathetic.**

Jay and I both desire the state of success. Starting from scratch may be necessary to prompt him. Remember that the effectiveness of our teaching is equal to the response we receive. If we have caused a negative state, such as frustration, fear, or apathy, it is high time to make some kind of change.

I know from my focus-time rule that I must be changing states when my time is up according to the age of my students. When that appears to be too long, and I can tell by the behavior in the classroom, I need to create more timely state changes. On an individual basis, I can use my knowledge of learning styles to deal with the student. Look at Figure 8.1 and the learning loop.

If a student becomes frustrated and falls out of the learning loop, the teacher must get him or her back on as soon as possible. First, check to see how many students appear frustrated. If there are several, it may be of value to simply try a different strategy with the whole class. If there are only a few who don't get it, putting students in small groups and working on the concept that way might help. It might be helpful to put the frustrated students together and work with them as the others practice the concept. When it comes down to a one-on-one situation, figuring out what modality preference the student has may be the answer.

Brian is in the third grade and is having a problem with division. He approaches the teacher:

Brian: I just don't *see* what to do with what's left over.

Teacher: Brian, didn't you *hear* what I said about remainders?

Brian: It *looks* like something's wrong when I *picture* it.

Teacher: You need to practice your listening skills. It should be *clear as a bell* for a student like you.

Once the teacher becomes aware of modality preferences and understands Brian's learning style, the conversation changes:

Brian: This doesn't *look* right to me.

Teacher: Brian, let me *show* you how this is done. *Watch* carefully.

Brian: Oh, yeah, I *see* what you mean.

Teacher: I knew you'd *get the picture* quickly.

Figure 8.1 Learning Loop

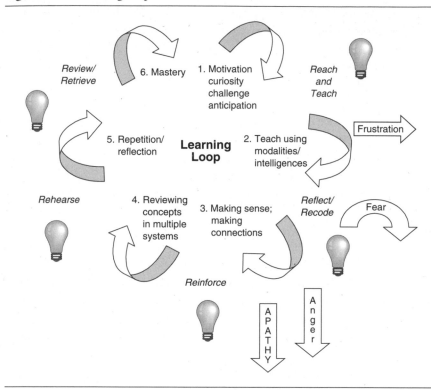

NOTE: Starting with a positive state, such as curiosity, the lesson is developed through various modalities. If students fail to stay in the loop until they achieve mastery, they generally become frustrated with the initial teaching strategies or they see no significance in the lesson. It is important to get them back in the loop during this process. Otherwise, rehearsal and review will be meaningless and make things more difficult.

What is so impressive about the procedure is that it is easy. The skill involved in managing the states of others and speaking to their preferred learning styles aids learning and relationships. Brian was saved from entering the state of fear and possibly apathy. His self-esteem was kept intact, and his relationship with his teacher was positive.

> If we want our students to learn what we are teaching, we must be aware of their states and manage them.

We are constantly acquiring information about the world around us. When we talk to someone who is not paying attention to us, that person is paying attention to *something*. Information is always being acquired. If we want our students to learn what we are teaching, we must be aware of their states and manage them.

Things to Remember

1. A state is a feeling we have that is a combination of our emotions, thoughts, and physiology.

2. All behavior is connected to state.

3. What we do at any moment in time depends on our state.

States to Encourage

The positive learning states include curiosity, anticipation, and challenge. When you can recognize these states and elicit them, the classroom runs more smoothly, and more learning takes place. There are certainly other states, but these are critical. When you have aroused curiosity in your classroom, your students may have their eyebrows raised (visual), their heads tilted (auditory), or be leaning forward (kinesthetic). Anticipation usually creates students who are sitting up straight with their eyebrows raised (visual), talking excitedly with their heads tilted (auditory), and moving a bit with their bodies leaning into the learning arena (kinesthetic). Some learners will be looking around alertly (visual), talking confidently and excitedly (auditory), and moving rapidly when challenged (kinesthetic). See Table 8.1 for a list of states and their identifiers.

State Changes and Classroom Management

According to *Classroom Instruction That Works* (Marzano, Pickering, & Pollack, 2001), a meta-analysis suggests that how aware we are of what is going on in our classrooms makes a big difference in how that classroom runs. Another factor is emotional objectivity, which is a result of taking care of ourselves. Because our students can be in different states at any one time, it is imperative that we learn to manage and elicit certain states. We try to keep them at the same emotional level. We want their attention. In order to do this, we must be "with it," that is, aware of what is going on in the classroom. We also must be able to be objective with these students and keep our own emotions under control and out of the way of our interactions with students.

The following list includes ways to do this that add to the learning experience rather than detract from it. We want to change our students' states and put them in a positive learning state.

Switch roles. Ask a student to come to the front of the class and reteach any part of the lesson. Students are curious to observe their peers and often attend carefully to find mistakes.

Table 8.1 Brain States and Their Identifiers According to Modalities

Brain States	Visual Characteristics	Auditory Characteristics	Kinesthetic Characteristics
Curiosity	Looking around, squinting, sitting up very straight	Asking questions	Moving about
Anticipation	Leaning forward with eyes wide open	Moving head from side to side, asking questions	Wiggling or jumping in seat
Challenge	Sitting up very straight, looking to gather information, eyes determined	Speaking loudly, asking for information	Moving purposefully, gathering materials and/or people to help
Frustration	Looking around anxiously	Shaking head, mumbling, may be asking questions	Clenched teeth, heavy movements, strong tapping or rocking
Fear	No eye contact, hiding	Shaking head, hiding, mumbling	Hiding, less movement
Anger	Nasty look, rolling eyes	Tight mouth, yelling	Walking away, hitting something
Apathy	Not looking around, eyes glazed, slumped in chair	Not listening, could be talking to self	Shoulders slumped, arms crossed

Stand up. Asking students to stand while you present information for a few minutes quickly changes their physiology and their state. It will change their breathing and cause the release of neurotransmitters such as serotonin, dopamine, and norepinephrine. These aid in learning.

Breathing. Ask your students to take deep breaths. This will change their physical state and give much-needed oxygen to the brain to help them learn.

Put on some background music. While you are speaking, walk slowly to your boom box and play some low-volume music. Continue the lesson. This change will arouse your students.

Change your teaching spot. If your students have to move in their seats to see you or watch something you are doing, that simple movement may change their states and bring them back on task. (I have actually walked over to a table and stood on it! That really got their attention!)

Call for consensus. Simply stop where you are and ask, "All those who agree with what I just said raise your hands." The students who are off task will quickly realize something is going on when they see or feel the rush of hands being raised.

Repeat what I said. Say "Turn to the person on your left and repeat my last sentence." The movement and the realization that they may have been "spacing out" will bring them back.

Some state changes may have to be more drastic and do take away from the learning momentarily. This may be necessary if the other changes aren't effective. You can send the students for drinks of water, stretch, play "Simon Sez" (I always played "Sprenger Sez"), tell a story, tell a joke, or change seats.

Keep in mind that you are managing the emotional states of your students. This is the most important job you have. The emotional-learning connection is the key to helping our students learn and remember.

MUSIC

Music can be used in a variety of ways, and recent research suggests that music will help with reading. At Stanford University, a study implied that musical training can improve the spoken word. Musicians appear to have an easier time distinguishing between rapidly changing sounds (Sturrock, 2005). It has also been found that music is as much a motor function as it is an auditory one (Cromie, 2001). That's probably why even when we think about a melody, we start to move our bodies a little. This

Music is known to help release emotions.

is great news to add to the recent information on movement helping the brain. Music is known to help release emotions (Pert, 1997). It also is a valuable tool, because every song has a beginning and an end. Each of these can be used as a cue for managing the classroom.

Music and Emotion

Research has shown that music causes the brain to release endorphins, the body's own pain reliever. When there is no pain and endorphins are released, the body experiences a pleasurable feeling. To prove this, endorphin blockers were given to an experimental group. When their favorite music was played, they indicated that they did not get the same good feelings they usually did and therefore did not enjoy the music as much (Jourdain, 1997).

You know those silly-looking people who drive alone in their cars and dance around in their seats as they sing along with the radio? I am one of those people. I listen to the oldies on my way to work, and I feel great. In the past, I would get to school, do some of my work, and wait for my students. Their music would always be playing when they entered the room. Some of them would be dancing and singing to the music, but I was not. I discovered that I wasn't playing music that was good for me. I needed to be pumped up just like the kids. So, I changed my opening music to put myself in a positive state.

I realized that whatever music I played, the kids would get used to it and become anchored to it. Anchoring is attaching an emotion or memory to certain music. I needed music that I already had a good anchor to so it would get me into the right teaching state. I switched from the Disney music I had been playing to some Beach Boys and Beatles music I loved. It made a tremendous difference in how I started my day. My students became attached to the music and felt their day was enhanced when it was played. It was not only a ritual, as described in Chapter 4, but also a way to get all of us into positive states.

Brain Waves

Music affects the brain by releasing endorphins and also affecting brain waves. The electricity in the brain is measured in waves. Most researchers work with the four major types of brain waves: delta, theta, alpha, and beta. These waves can be measured with an **electroencephalogram (EEG).** The speed and regularity of the waves can determine the type of learning that is occurring. Each wave is very different.

Delta. This is the brain wave seen during sleep. These waves cycle 1 to 3 times per second. No conscious learning is taking place during sleep. The brain is firing very slowly. Many researchers believe that this is the time when the brain cleans house; in other words, useless information is disposed of. Current research suggests that the rehearsal of new memories is also occurring. Some studies of rats while they were learning and again during sleep suggest that the learning patterns were repeated while they slept (Wilson & McNaughton, 1994). They appeared to actually be practicing the maze they had been taught!

Theta. This brain wave usually occurs twice during the night. The brain is cycling just a little faster than when delta waves are seen, at about 4 to 7 times per second. This is a very relaxed state that usually cannot be achieved on a conscious level. Some people can achieve this state through meditation and other forms of relaxation. It is said that this state is very receptive to learning. Perhaps the "sleep learning" records of the 1950s were a result of a belief that the theta state was accessible throughout the night. Unfortunately, the records did not work. The theta state occurs just as you are falling asleep. It's that dreamy feeling as you drift off. It also occurs as you are waking. If you wake to a clock radio and a song is playing, you may find yourself singing or humming that song all day. In the theta state, your brain may have absorbed that learning quickly and easily.

Alpha. This brain wave cycles about 8 to 12 times per second. This is still a relaxed state, but it can be accessed much more easily than theta. The alpha state is a state of relaxed alertness. Many believe that it facilitates learning and heightens memory. The alpha state can be accessed through specific types of baroque music. This music has 40 to 60 beats per minute. The music tends to slow

I always play baroque music during tutoring sessions and parent conferences.

down respiration, heart rate, and also brain waves. In so doing, the music causes relaxation and helps many out of stressful situations. I always play baroque music during tutoring sessions and parent conferences.

Beta. I call beta waves the "run, see, go, do" waves. These are the waves that get me up in the morning; they are cycling from 12 to 40 times per second. Some researchers believe that these are the waves we need for new learning and new memory. When you are talking and figuring out problems, you are using beta waves. Beta waves go beyond relaxed alertness to full attentiveness. New research suggests that time is very limited in this state and we must use it wisely.

Your brain always has several different types of waves. However, one of these waves will be dominant. Remember, this electrical activity determines the speed at which the neurons are firing—that is, "talking to each other." When we are in a hyper state at times, there may be some confusion. Some call this *super beta* because the neurons fire more than 40 cycles per second. Unusual electrical activity has been attributed to some types of seizures. This very important brain function must find a delicate balance to aid in our learning and living.

As educators, we can use this information to our advantage. Music affects brain waves. When we want our students to relax and slow down, we can play music that has fewer beats per minute. Baroque music, which was composed between 1600 and 1750, is known to do this. One must be somewhat cautious, because not all baroque music meets the requirement of having around 60 beats per minute. Look for the word **adagio** on the selection. This indicates a slower piece.

I always use baroque selections at testing time to reduce test anxiety, but it can also be used in other situations. After lunch, when my students sometimes come to the classroom wound up from recess, I often play this music to calm them. For the late afternoon study period, when students are more likely to want to talk than work, baroque music can also be helpful.

Because teamwork is a large part of my classroom practice, music also helps me rouse my teams for action. For brainstorming and problem solving, I want music that is faster than baroque because the students require beta waves for this work. I usually play a classical piece for this, by composers such as Mozart or Beethoven.

The music affects students' levels of arousal, which affects the states they are in. I may begin a lesson with the theme

The music affects students' levels of arousal, which affects the states they are in.

from the movie *Jaws* to perk their curiosity. For challenge, I may play the theme from *Mission Impossible.* Before we leave the building for recess or PE, I can play "Walk in the Sunshine" by *The Brady Bunch.* In these ways, I can use music to elicit the state I desire for my students and help them handle their emotions.

Music for Management

The music playing as my students enter the room affects their states and also helps with classroom management. When the music stops, my students know it is time to be quiet and in their seats, because class is going to begin. I also have a "call back" song for my classes. If they are working on an activity and I want them to wind it up and be ready to share information, I play the song. They know that when it is over, they should be in their seats and ready. This same song can be used to send them out for drinks or for pencil sharpening.

If I want students to clean up quickly, I will play the theme from *The Lone Ranger* (the *William Tell* "Overture"). All cleanups must be complete by the time the song is over. At the end of the day, when it is time to gather homework materials and put school supplies away, I may play "Happy Trails," by Roy Rogers or "Wonderful World," by Louis Armstrong. These songs pleasantly prepare them for the trip home and give them a positive feeling about school.

There are many other ways to use music. It takes only imagination, a cassette or CD player, and some music. Music can be downloaded from the Internet, purchased inexpensively, or if you are lucky as I have been, donated by students and parents. You probably have your own music library at home with selections you can use in your classroom.

Table 8.2 shows a child's musical capabilities at various ages. Keep in mind that every child is different. This is information based on the book *Music With the*

Table 8.2   Developing Musical Abilities

Age	Musical Abilities	Things to Do
From 20 weeks after conception	Hears sounds	Sing; read poetry and nursery rhymes.
At birth	Hears high-pitched noises, may be calmed by lower sounds and can locate sound in front of them	Sing or play simple songs, lullabies, and nursery rhymes.
Three months	Responds physically to music by moving and making sounds	Sing or play simple songs, lullabies, and nursery rhymes.
Six months	Imitates sounds	Sing or play simple songs, lullabies, and nursery rhymes.
Eighteen months to three years	Distinguishes between loud and quiet, fast and slow, aware of beat and rhythm, learns simple songs, plays simple instruments	Dance with them to music; play with bells; clap.
Three to five years	Is more aware of pitch, can play more instruments	Use drums and shakers; play clapping games; dance.
Five to seven years	Has new vocal ranges, better memory of music through repetition, time for percussion instruments	Begin music lessons; continue to play clapping and rhyming games.
Seven to eleven years	Can begin composing, may want to learn to play an instrument	Begin or encourage music lessons; sing.
Eleven to fourteen years	Can sing with vocal expression, may play more instruments, develop a musical identity	Play a variety of music styles; continue or begin lessons.
Fourteen years and beyond	May be interested in a musical career	Continue musical encouragement.

Brain in Mind by Eric Jensen (2000d) and the British Broadcasting Company's Web site Parents Music Room (http://www.bbc.co.uk/music/ parents/).

MANAGING MOVEMENT

Small children learn through movement. Kinesthetic learners learn through movement. Bodily/kinesthetic intelligence involves movement. Movement aids procedural memory. If these aren't enough reasons to add movement to the classroom, let's try these:

- Movement helps with reading.
- Movement gets oxygen-rich blood and glucose to the brain.
- Movement changes states.
- Movement offers a change of pace when our neurons are tired and overworked from doing an activity too long.
- Movement is fun!

There are two reasons most teachers restrict movement in their classrooms:

1. They don't know how to use movement for learning.

2. They're afraid of losing control of the class.

If we want our classrooms to run smoothly and to lower our students' stress levels and our own, movement is a way to do it. So, the question is—how?

Table 8.3 offers you some ideas for planned movement to energize and movement for learning content. These are state changers, learning opportunities, and stress reducers!

THE WICKED WITCH IS DEAD

Okay, maybe she's not really dead, but she's definitely under control. By more effectively managing my classroom, I handled my stress levels and those of my students. Of course, there can still be days when the witch tries to show herself. I know that I must look around my room to see whose brain is doing its best to create that stress. Rather than doling out punishment, I know this is the student who needs special attention. Before giving it, I use my music and state management to carefully adjust the tone of my classroom.

Table 8.3   Movement Activities

Movement for Energizing	Movement for Learning
Change seats.	Walk while reading, slowing down for punctuation marks.
Find someone who . . . has a birthday close to yours.	Create a specific movement for each different punctuation mark.
Play music, and have students stand up, turn around, sit down, and open their books before the music ends.	Toss a bean bag among students; have them answer the previous question and ask a new one with each toss.
Stand on one foot.	Role-play.
Run in place for 30 seconds.	Find different angles in the school building.
Give high fives to three people.	Hold a relay race that involves writing as many vocabulary words as you can think of related to a topic.
Stand up and take three deep breaths.	Think-pair-share: Have students stand, find a partner, and share what has been studied so far.
Play "Simon Sez."	Play "Simon Sez for Learning," e.g., "Simon says if there are nine planets touch your toes."
March to music.	Remember a list using movements as cues.
Cross laterals: Have students stand and cross their midline by touching hands to opposite knees.	Form shapes with your body.
Play "Musical Chairs."	Measure with your hands.
Skip across the room.	Go on field trips.
Stretch.	Find a partner, walk around the room, and discuss the posters on the wall. Find your favorite.
Bunny hop.	Make a human graph: If you agree, go to this side of the room, If you disagree, go to the other side.

Jay is at it again. I am trying to explain to the teams how they are to continue with their projects. I glance at the clock and realize they have been listening to my voice for about 13 minutes. I can either reprimand Jay or try a state change for the entire class. If Jay is jumpy, there are probably others who are also feeling the same way.

I slip over to the boom box as I continue talking and start playing "The Hokey Pokey." The eighth graders quickly stand, and for two minutes, we are all "turning ourselves around." When the music ends, I finish my instructions, and the teams get busy. Jay is back on task. I stay close to his team to be sure he understands the instructions and is doing his part. If he needs help, I am there.

Long live the Good Witch!

We're Off to See . . .

With a toolbox filled with strategies, our next leg of the journey is a snapshot of children in the classroom. We'll take a look at nutrition, sleep, and exercise. Unique brains will also be discussed. Do you have students in your classroom who are depressed, are bipolar, have attention-deficit issues, or suffer from learned helplessness? How do you recognize these, and what can you do about it? Chapter 9 offers some possibilities.

WIZDOM

Key Points to Ponder

1. Brain states can be managed or changed.

2. Music can be used to manage states, carry information, or arouse attention.

3. Movement is vital to learning and making connections in the brain.

Suggestions

- Managing and eliciting states make teaching much easier. Discipline problems almost disappear as your state changes keep the class moving at an enjoyable pace. Practice state changes in your classroom.

- Music can be used in several ways: as a carrier of information for automatic and emotional memory, as a way to control your students' arousal states (quiet them down or speed them up), and for classroom management. Check out this music Web site: http://www.musica.uci.edu/.
- Music will intrigue both your auditory learners and your learners with high musical/rhythmic intelligence. Let them participate in putting music programs together for you to enhance a unit or theme. It is rare that these students get to use their musical expertise in the classroom.
- Take care of your own personal needs. The less stressed you are, the easier it is to recognize the needs of your students.

9 **Dorothy**

Every Brain Is Unique

It must be inconvenient to be made of flesh, for you must sleep and eat and drink. However, you have brains, and it is worth a lot of bother to be able to think properly.

—The Scarecrow

My daughter, Marnie, is in second grade when the first call comes. It is her teacher, Miss Hill. "I'm having a little trouble with Marnie. She won't sit quietly in her seat." Marnie hasn't been able to "sit" anywhere. I think back to our car trips with her as a baby and toddler. She kicked and screamed throughout every trip; she couldn't stand to be confined in a car seat. "We'll talk to her and take care of it," I reply.

Scott laughs when I tell him about the call. "We can't get her to sit still long enough to have dinner with us! How are we going to make her sit in a desk all day? Doesn't that teacher know that kids need to move?"

We try talking to Marnie. We tell her how she has to work this out. If her teacher wants her to stay in her seat, then she has to do so.

About two weeks later, the phone rings. It is Miss Hill. "Mrs. Sprenger, is there something wrong with Marnie? She keeps falling off of her chair."

Immediately, my mind goes back to the dining room. Sitting still at dinnertime was a battle in her younger days. Marnie would move around so much on the dining room chair that she would often lose center and fall off!

"Miss Hill, I think Marnie is having trouble sitting for long periods. She is moving around on her chair and losing her balance." The woman probably thinks I am crazy, but she seems to accept my explanation.

As the years go by, there are many phone calls. Marnie can't sit. Marnie isn't turning in her work. Marnie's desk is messy. It gets to the point where Scott and I flip a coin to see who has to go to Marnie's conferences. They tell us she is a happy, delightful child.

She doesn't really cause trouble.... If only she would sit and work like the other kids. If only she would pay attention in class. We are sick of the complaints.

By high school, Marnie figures it out. In 10 minutes in almost any class, she can start to daydream or fall asleep.

During Marnie's sophomore year in high school, I am traveling for the state board of education. I call home each evening. It is midweek, and Marnie answers the phone. She is congested from a cold and cough.

"Marnie, you'd better take care of yourself. Take some vitamin C, drink plenty of fluids, and get some sleep!"

Her reply says it all. "Don't worry, Mom, I'm getting plenty of sleep. I'm sleeping in history. I'm sleeping in chemistry, I'm sleeping in English!"

Josh, our older child, did well in the traditional setting. We always said he knew how to play the education game. Marnie just didn't have the rulebook for that game. Here were two kids with similar genes, the same parents, and yet very different brains. Even with the same environment, we have two unique individuals with unique brains. What do those brains have in common? Do they have the same basic needs?

THE CARE AND FEEDING OF DOROTHY'S BRAIN

Dorothy's experience in Oz indicates that she has a very adaptive brain. Her ability to handle her new situation and solve problems is based on the patterns previously stored in her brain. What does it take to have a healthy brain that can easily find patterns and solve problems?

It's easy to begin with some basics: oxygen, water, glucose, protein, and sleep. About every fourth heartbeat provides needed sustenance for this three-pound organ. Blood carries the necessary oxygen, water, glucose, and protein. Thirst is an indication that the level of water in the blood is low. Dehydration quickly causes havoc in the brain. It can dramatically affect attention. Students should be allowed access to water on a constant or consistent basis. Some teachers are reluctant about having water available in the classroom, because they fear the novelty will be detrimental to the learning process. It really doesn't take long for the novelty to wear off, and the presence of water bottles or coolers becomes part of the learning environment.

Brain Food

Dorothy's brain needs proper nutrients. As educators, we cannot be in control of what our students consume; however, we can be good role models and share with parents the proper diet for a healthy body and brain. The most important meal of the day may very well be the first. Studies have shown that students who eat a balanced breakfast including protein, fat, starch, and sugar perform better. They may have better attention, fewer mistakes, faster retrieval of information, and better concentration (Bergmann, 2005).

Many students skip breakfast, which may very well be detrimental to learning. Since the brain cannot store energy, it is running on fumes when you first awaken. The brain needs glucose to expend energy and send those messages.

Here's some interesting information:

- According to the State of Minnesota Breakfast Study, students who ate breakfast before starting school had a general increase in math grades and reading scores, increased attention, reduced nurse visits, and improved behaviors (Bergmann, 2005).
- Children who eat a healthy breakfast "meet their daily nutritional needs, keep their weight under control, have lower blood cholesterol levels, attend school more frequently, and make fewer trips to the school nurse's office complaining of tummy aches" ("Kids and," 2003).
- Kids who eat breakfast are more likely than children who skip breakfast to consume foods with adequate levels of minerals, such as calcium, phosphorus, magnesium; and vitamins, such as riboflavin, vitamins A, C, and B12, and folate ("Kids and," 2003).

Dr. Marian Diamond (1999b), famed neuroscience researcher from the University of California, Berkeley, and others (Carper, 2000; Howard, 2006; Whitaker, 1999) offer many nutrition suggestions to aid the brain.

Vitamin B1 helps the brain use glucose and promotes the release of neurotransmitters. Food sources include green leafy vegetables, citrus fruits, and pasta.

Vitamin B6 aids in the metabolism of amino acids, which are the building blocks of neurotransmitters. Potatoes, bananas, turkey, and whole grains are good food sources.

Vitamin B12 helps build red blood cells and aids memory. Two good sources are tuna and liver.

Calpain works to keep connections between neurons clean. Dairy products provide calpain.

Choline is the precursor to acetylcholine, the neurotransmitter involved in forming long-term memories. Tofu, soybeans, egg yolks, and peanuts are sources of choline.

Vitamin E improves memory by improving circulation and adding oxygen to the brain. Although this vitamin may be found in foods, 200-IU supplements are often recommended.

Magnesium improves memory and is found in dark green leafy vegetables, peanuts, and bananas.

Potassium is necessary to transmit messages. Bananas, green leafy vegetables, and potatoes are sources of this substance.

In general, those who are getting a balanced diet and an appropriate number of calories each day are probably getting most of the necessary nutrients. However, many of our students make unwise food choices and need to be guided in their eating habits. As primary role models for our students, we must model good nutrition. This might mean forgoing that can of soda that may sit on our desk during the day. We can also discuss our food choices and the fact that we begin our day with a healthy breakfast. Considering the growing number of eating disorders, it behooves us to not mention any diet we may be currently following. Eating well and exercising should be the messages we send to our students and to their parents. A chart of the basic food groups may be a proper peripheral for the classroom. As students' eyes wander around the room, their brains may absorb this pertinent information in a nonconscious manner.

As primary role models for our students, we must model good nutrition.

Sugar can aid in memory. Studies show that 30 minutes after candy is eaten, brain glucose levels are high. This could help in a testing situation because we know the brain requires glucose; however, an hour and a half later blood sugar has dropped, and the student will be at a disadvantage (Ratey, 2000). If students eat foods with refined sugar before and during school, their brains overall will not function well. Several studies suggest that students on high-sugar diets score lower on IQ tests. Some also have mood swings and earn low grades (Carper, 2000).

Protein is essential to the brain. Digestion causes protein to be broken down into amino acids that make up many of the brain's neurotransmitters. It is important to have protein at each meal; however, an excessive amount is not healthy. Three or four small servings are sufficient (Whitaker, 1999). Students often eat a disproportionate amount of carbohydrates. Because carbohydrates cause the release of serotonin, sleepiness may be a result of this excess. It may be best to encourage students to save those carbohydrates for after school, when they don't need to be attentive.

Presently there are excellent books available that support the idea that some basic foods are good for your brain and for overall health. I would be remiss if I did not mention these foods in this book. One important component of many of these brain foods is their antioxidant properties. To give you a picture of the importance of antioxidants, think of an apple slice that has been sitting out for quite awhile. It's not very

Antioxidants rid our brains of the leftover free radicals.

pretty, as it has changed from white to brown. That's oxidation taking place. Oxygen, in the form of molecules called free radicals, is a by-product of our brain function, and these molecules can cause deterioration in the brain much like that of oxygen on the apple slice. Imagine your brain rusting away from the free radical oxygen molecules! This is why antioxidants are so important. They rid our brains of these leftovers.

The myelin coating on the axons of our brain is a lipid. Lipids are fats that are constructed from omega-3 fatty acids. Many of the recommended foods are rich in these fats. Our Western lifestyle has included foods high in omega-6 fatty acids. These are necessary as well, but not in the amounts that we generally consume. It takes a delicate balance of these fats for optimal brain functioning (see Table 9.1).

SLEEP AND THE BRAIN

My first-hour class has the lowest scores of my five classes. As I look at my grade book, I see that they turn in less homework than any of my other groups. And they never get involved in discussions. I really am tired of trying to get them interested in learning. They don't even seem to hear my music! I ask the other teachers what their experiences are with this group. The science teacher can't believe that we're talking about the same group of students. They come to her fifth hour, and they have the highest scores in the seventh grade. The math teacher agrees that they are very bright, but he also has some problems keeping them quiet. Quiet! I can't even get them to speak at all!

As we continue to compare notes, the social studies teacher starts complaining about her first-hour eighth-grade class. "They are awfully well behaved, but I can't get a discussion going with them. I may as well be on video with the lack of response I get."

The fifth-grade French teacher pipes up, "My first-hour class is like that, too. It's very difficult to tell if they have the vocabulary. It's as if they're still asleep!"

Table 9.1   Brain Food: Remember, What Is Good for the Body Is Good for the Brain

Healthy Food	Why
Blueberries	Often called "brain berries." This fruit is packed with antioxidants.
Oranges	Rich in Vitamin C, potassium, and folates.
Salmon	Good for your brain and your heart. This is one fish not to be missed, as it is rich in omega-3 fatty acids. These will help with those connections in your brain as well as help overcome depression.
Spinach	Popeye was right. Spinach is loaded with vitamins, minerals, and omega-3 fatty acids.
Tomatoes	Pizza sauce, spaghetti sauce, and ketchup are made from tomatoes, and you can derive the same benefits from them! Lycopene, potassium, B vitamins, and vitamin C are all included in this wonderful food. And here's some powerful evidence for their importance: Remember, previously, I mentioned the nun study and Dr. Snowdon? Interestingly enough, the nuns who were most able to care for themselves had the highest concentration of lycopene in their bloodstreams!
Turkey	Rich in vitamins and minerals including B6, B12, iron, selenium, and zinc. Turkey also contains tryptophan, which is the precursor to the feel-good neurotransmitter, serotonin.
Nuts	Another precursor to serotonin. Contain magnesium, potassium, vitamin B6, and omega-3 fatty acids.
Olive oil	Contains omega-3 fatty acids. It's a much healthier choice than vegetable oil.
Yogurt	Contains vitamin B2, B12, zinc, magnesium, calcium.
Chocolate	Best news yet! Dark, cocoa-based chocolate increases the release of dopamine.

SOURCE: Adapted from *You: The Owner's Manual* (Roizen & Oz, 2005) and *Super Foods r/x* (Pratt & Matthews, 2004)

Sleep deprivation is a major problem in our society. It was believed that these problems did not exist until adolescence, but recent studies show that prior to puberty, children are starting to sleep less. It is believed that children under 10 years old require 9 to 11 hours of sleep. They generally fall asleep easily and are energetic throughout the day. When adolescence begins, our students need 9 hours and 15 minutes of sleep (Dement & Vaughan, 1999).

Sleep deprivation is a major problem in our society.

Sleep deprivation can cause significant problems. The ability to learn and remember can be hampered. Accidents are more likely to happen. A lack of sleep can contribute to depression, and some sleep-starved children exhibit characteristics of attention deficit disorder or hyperactivity. In some cases, students are simply overscheduled. There aren't enough hours in the day for all their activities. Unfortunately, it is sleep time that is taken away (Kelly, 2000).

Brown University researchers recently studied the sleep habits and school performance of children. The study participants included 39 boys and 35 girls from the ages of 6½ to 12¾. First the children tracked their own sleep for a week in order to obtain a baseline. Then the students were divided into two groups: a restricted sleep group and an optimized sleep group. After another week the groups switched. So, in three weeks each one had a baseline sleep schedule, an optimized sleep schedule, and a restricted sleep schedule. At the end of each week, teachers rated each student on the following criteria: academic problems, hyperactivity, anxiety, sadness, emotional problems, illness, oppositional-aggressive behavior, attention and concentration problems, and sleepiness. When students slept less, they were rated as sleepier and had more attention and concentration problems. Normal sleep and optimal sleep resulted in fewer schoolwork problems (Fallone, Acebo, Seifer, & Carskadon, 2005).

Many of our middle school students are sleep deprived by the time they enter sixth grade. As a result, their attention and concentration may be affected. Why aren't our students getting enough sleep? There may be a relationship between lack of sleep and bedtime enforcement (Bower, 2000). Changes in the brain at adolescence change the biological clock, a cluster of neurons that sends signals throughout the body and controls fundamentally all the internal operations. These changes may be occurring at a younger age in some students than was previously thought. One of the operations involved in the change is sleep. The time at which melatonin, the chemical released to induce sleep, is distributed in the brain suddenly becomes later, so these students are not ready for sleep. Add to that the desire to be more independent, the need to control one's own life, and the fact that older teenagers work late hours—and a problem exists. What's more, those chemicals needed for sleep are still in the bodies of older students during first-hour class. The schools in Edina, Minnesota, changed their starting time from 7:25 a.m. to 8:30 a.m.; this resulted in better grades, higher test scores, and happier teachers and students (University of Minnesota, 1997).

The brain needs sleep to dispose of trivial data and practice new information (Dement & Vaughan, 1999). Sleep also appears to be necessary to regulate emotions, and emotions are already a problem for the adolescent age group. This combination may contribute to the recent increase in violence among this age group (Carskadon, 1995). If sleep deprivation is becoming more universal in that it includes students in primary grades, will we be seeing lower test scores and more emotional upheavals?

Changing starting times would be helpful. A later starting time for middle- and upper-grade students would allow them to get more sleep. Short of that, be aware that your first-hour students may not perform as well as those in your other classes. Repetition and out-of-class work may be necessary for these students to stay on track. Rotating schedules will help this situation. I was involved in a rotating schedule for several years; both students and teachers loved it. This simply means starting Tuesday with second hour instead of first, Wednesday with third hour, and so on. In this way, it takes six or seven days before that first-hour class is back in your room at the beginning of the day. This is also an excellent way to see how students perform at different times of the day. Let's face it—last-hour classes can be a challenge for teachers and students. If you have a self-contained classroom, you have some control over what is covered in the early morning.

Very young students may be negatively affected by a later starting time. Their biological clocks have not changed as dramatically as the adolescents' clocks, and they have a tendency to awaken early. Positive effects have been seen in studies of elementary schools that made their starting times earlier. Students appear to be more alert throughout the day and eager to learn (Kubow, Wahlstrom, & Bemis, 1999). The two to three hours they may spend at home before school may be their most attentive time.

Very young students may be negatively affected by a later starting time.

What about naps? Researchers say that napping for up to 45 minutes can be helpful. Beyond that amount of time, a full two hours is suggested, so the body can go through a complete sleep cycle (Brink, 2000). Remember that this is only playing catch-up. Is it time to initiate a siesta period at school?

This is another area in which we must be role models. Rather than sharing the fact that we did not get enough sleep, we should be promoting good sleep habits. We should be proud of getting the eight hours of sleep we need rather than boast that we require so little to operate.

EXERCISE

About 20 minutes of exercise makes you less likely to contract up to 50 different diseases. It reduces the likelihood by only about one percent (Sapolsky, 1999), but what an easy and important way to take care of yourself! Almost everything we read tells us how important exercise is for our bodies. What does it do for our brain? In the past few years, science has recognized that the brain grows new neurons. The process, neurogenesis, continues throughout life. Exercise encourages this process by increasing blood flow to the brain. As the blood flow increases, new blood vessels develop to adequately handle the supply. The increased blood vessels act as insurance. If some of the vessels are damaged or blocked, there are others to take over their duties. This decreases the likelihood of further damage. Remember that blood provides all the nutrients the brain needs. So, from exercise we have more blood and more nutrients to keep the brain growing. Studies of rats found that with more complex exercise, more blood vessels and more nerve cells developed (Ratey, 2000).

At the same time, exercise serves another function. The increase in nutrients and oxygen also helps the brain rid itself of debris. The glial cells that serve the purpose of digesting parts of dead cells are able to do this more easily. Exercise also causes the brain to release other important nutrients called growth factors. Several studies suggest that the growth factor, brain-derived neurotropic factor (BDNF), is released after voluntary exercise. This substance actually can increase cognition, as it helps with neuronal communication (Stern & Carstensen, 2000). William Greenough, at the University of Illinois, experimented with rats and exercise. One group of animals ran across ropes and bridges, and another group ran on an automated wheel. A third group remained sedentary. The group that needed the precise movements for the ropes and bridges had a greater number of connections among neurons in their brains than either of the other two groups (Hannaford, 2005).

There are many health benefits from exercise. Reducing depression is one of them. This probably relates to the release of the neurotransmitters that affect mood, serotonin and dopamine, and

There are many health benefits from exercise.

the decrease of the stress hormone cortisol. Sleep is often enhanced as well (Giuffre & DiGeronimo, 1999). Memory function may improve as a result of these benefits.

How much activity is enough? Thirty minutes per day at least three or four days per week is usually recommended. The more organized, challenging, and well executed this movement is, the more beneficial it will be. If your school does not provide physical education classes, recess may be the only time for proper movement. Recesses should be at least 30 minutes long. Short recesses may excite kids and leave them overaroused. Concentration could be hampered. Of course, recesses shouldn't be so long that students have little energy left afterward (Jensen, 2000c).

Figure 9.1 is a reproducible chart for your students to keep track of their eating, sleeping, and exercising habits. Have them fill this chart out for several weeks, and discuss what they can do to improve their overall health and learning.

UNIQUE BRAINS, UNIQUE LEARNERS

There are many unique brains, including addicted brains, autistic brains, anxious brains, attention deficit brains, behavior-disordered brains, depressive brains, dyslexic brains, epileptic brains, fetal alcohol syndrome and fetal alcohol-affected brains, helpless brains, hyperactive brains, impoverished brains, obsessive-compulsive brains, oppositional brains, sleep-deprived brains, and traumatized brains.

Providing information on all of these brains would take at least one other book, so I am going to focus on three. Depression is becoming a major problem and recognition of it is vital. Learned helplessness and attention deficit are issues that teachers are faced with every day, and having information about how to recognize and teach these brains made quite a difference for me.

The Depressive Brain

As educators, we must be extremely aware and concerned about depression in our students. Emerging research suggests that even mild depression from which there is complete recovery may cause permanent damage to the hippocampus (Restak, 2000). This structure is vital to factual memory. Therefore it is very important to be aware of the signs of depression to ensure that our students receive expeditious and effective treatments.

People with depression find little pleasure in their lives and see the world in a distorted or negative way. The symptoms of depression may include the following:

- Sadness or irritability that persists
- Low self-esteem or feelings of worthlessness

Figure 9.1 The Care and Feeding of My Brain

Week of _____	Hours of Sleep	What I Had for Breakfast	What I Had for Lunch	What I Had for Dinner	What I Did for Exercise
Sunday					
Monday					
Tuesday					
Wednesday					
Thursday					
Friday					
Saturday					

- Loss of interest in previously important and favorite things
- Change in appetite or sleep (either increase or decrease)
- Difficulty concentrating
- Physical pains that seem to have no cause, such as headaches and stomachaches
- Activity level changes—either more hyperactive or more lethargic
- Thoughts of death or suicide

The key to recognizing depressive problems is to watch for change. Any variation in a child's behavior that appears to have no external cause should be checked out. If a student has an obvious concern, such as a loss, divorce, or move, and you see a change that lasts for more than a few weeks, it should be considered a possible depression. Other mental disorders often accompany depression. Two possibilities are attention deficit disorder and eating disorders. These need to be treated along with the depressive disorder for effective treatment (National Institute of Mental Health, 2000).

The key to recognizing depressive problems is to watch for change.

There are certain risks associated with depression. Among them is an increased risk for illness. Depression suppresses the immune system just as stress does (as discussed in Chapter 3). It also increases the risk for substance abuse and suicidal behavior, especially in adolescents. Unfortunately, signs of depressive disorders in young people are often viewed as normal mood swings associated with a particular developmental stage.

Of American children, five percent may be depressed, according to the American Academy of Pediatrics (Jensen, 2000b). As you look at your class, ask yourself some questions about which students exhibit the following behaviors:

- Frequently absent?
- Performs poorly?
- Talks of or has tried to run away from home?
- Outbursts of shouting, complaining, unexplained irritability, or crying?
- Acts bored?
- Lack of interest in playing with friends?
- Signs of alcohol or substance abuse?
- Isolating themselves socially or trouble communicating?
- Expresses a fear of death?
- Extreme sensitivity to rejection or failure?
- Increased irritability, anger, or hostility?

- Reckless behavior?
- Difficulty with relationships?

The causes of depression are numerous and vary with each individual. Genetics can play a role. Those who are genetically prone to depression may secrete more cortisol during a stressful time, have an imbalance in their serotonin and norepinephrine systems, or have a glitch in the feedback loop that stops stress hormones from being released (Sapolsky, 2004). In this way, nature and nurture probably play somewhat equal roles. The environment may provide the stressors that cause any of the genetic propensities to be expressed.

Which areas of the brain are affected by depression? Some areas of the brain become overactive, whereas others become underactive. Overactive areas include the cingulate cortex, which locks attention on sad feelings. Sad memories are held by the lateral prefrontal lobe, and the thalamus stimulates the amygdala, the creator of negative emotions (Carter, 1998).

There may be decreased prefrontal cortex activity with increased activity in the limbic area of the brain. This combination often causes the depressive person to be moody and negative, with low energy and sleep and appetite problems. Because of the problems with dopamine and norepinephrine, this student would have trouble concentrating. An area known for serotonin fibers, the anterior cingulate, located behind the frontal lobes, may show increased activity along with the thalamus and the basal ganglia. A student with this condition may be sad, irritable, and stuck in negative thought patterns. Decreased prefrontal cortex activity with a change (increase or decrease) in temporal lobe activity could result in sadness, irritability, or even rage (Amen, 1998).

Fortunately, we don't see a large percentage of students with depression. However, the statistics are growing. More than 500,000 children in America take antidepressants. In the adolescent population, one in eight may be experiencing depression (National Institute of Mental Health, 2000).

In the adolescent population, one in eight may be experiencing depression.

As educators, we have the opportunity to observe children in different settings. If you find a student exhibiting symptoms of depression, seek help. Counselors, school psychologists, and parents need to be aware of a possible problem. After that, there are some provisions to make as a teacher. Creating a positive environment with social support and plenty of consistency may be helpful to the depressed student. Because the neurotransmitters that affect mood are generally at low levels in these students, providing movement and exercise may encourage their release. Perhaps a "walk and talk" in nice weather would provide a release of dopamine, serotonin, and endorphins. It would also provide some social support and a verbal outlet if the student wanted to talk. Combine the walk with academics. An example would be, "Today we are going outside for a walk and talk. You are to share three things with your partner: one concept you learned today in science, one question you need answered concerning another subject area, and one thing you are going to do to make yourself feel good today. After you and your partner have covered these areas, you may talk about anything you wish. Be finished and line up at the school doors in 15 minutes."

Treatment will vary with the individual and the type of depression. It is rare that depression improves without some kind of intervention. Often, both medication and talk therapy are necessary. Antidepressants may be prescribed for a short time until no longer needed.

Another illness in the same category as depression is manic depression. With this disorder, the student experiences depressive symptoms as described above but also has periods of mania with very different characteristics. Someone who is experiencing the manic phase will exhibit these characteristics:

- Abnormal or excessive elation
- Unusual irritability
- Decreased need for sleep
- Grandiose notions
- Increased talking
- Racing thoughts
- Increased sexual desire
- Markedly increased energy
- Poor judgment
- Inappropriate social behavior

Larry started drinking in sixth grade. His friends thought it was pretty cool. By eighth grade, Larry was drinking almost every weekend. In high school, his habit became daily, and he found that he had to keep increasing the amount that he was consuming. The parents of Larry's friends didn't want them hanging around with him, but they did anyway. By his junior year, Larry discovered that if he smoked marijuana, he got the same results he was after. He began smoking pot every day before school. His friends enabled him by driving him to remote places before school started, so Larry could get high. His friends did not indulge with him on a regular basis, but some joined in on weekends.

Larry started to slowly give up his friendships. An excellent student, his grades began to go down. His behavior was erratic, and although he was the best player on the basketball team, he was kicked off because he missed so many practices.

Larry managed to get most of his classwork done, and because he was so intelligent, he did pretty well on final exams and graduated from high school. He was admitted to a Big Ten school. Due to his excessive use of marijuana and a few other drugs, Larry skipped most of his classes, became quite reclusive, and was kicked out of school at the end of his freshman year.

When Larry returned to his hometown, he lived with his parents, continued his drug use, and began exhibiting some unusual behaviors. He was arrested for stealing a car. He already owned a car and his family was quite well off financially. When asked why he did such a thing, Larry's answer was, "I was just walking by and saw the keys in the car, so I decided to take a ride."

At this point, Larry's parents kicked him out of the house. They were trying a "tough love" approach to Larry's problems.

Shortly after this episode, Larry visited a friend and began explaining his recent conversations with God. His friend thought his visions were a result of his drug use. One day, he bought a guitar and told his friends and family that he could play. He would strum the guitar making terrible sounds and smile and think he was really playing songs.

The turning point came when Larry tried to commit suicide. He was hospitalized, and after significant testing, it was discovered that Larry did not just have an addiction to drugs, he was bipolar. His mania caused the religious conversations, the car stealing, and the guitar playing; his depression took him to the suicide attempt. After detoxification, medication, and therapy, it was discovered that this disorder had been plaguing him since he was a child, and his alcohol and drug use were attempts at self-medication. He didn't like the way he felt, and the drugs helped him get through the day.

Manic depression, often called bipolar disorder, can be difficult to spot, because the extreme behaviors are often attributed to moodiness that we are likely to see in an adolescent. It is always important to err on the side of caution. In other words, when in doubt, check the policy at your school and see who you can have the student talk to. These students often self-medicate using alcohol or drugs. They don't understand why they feel as they do, so they look for a way to compensate. Then they are thought to have a drug problem, and their real problem—depression or manic depression—is overlooked.

> Manic-depressive students don't understand why they feel as they do. They often self-medicate with drugs or alcohol.

Larry, by the way, is doing well. He eventually went back to college, graduated with honors, got married, and has children and a good job. He was lucky.

Many people overlooked or misread what was happening to him, and I was one of those people. I am so grateful that he managed to live long enough to find the solution to his problem. Larry is the reason that I feel this information is so important for teachers to have.

The Helpless Brain

Learned helplessness is a disorder in which cause and effect no longer connect in a child's brain. Students have been exposed to chronic failure and feel that nothing they do will have an effect on their situation. This is a learned condition, not a genetic one.

Research on psychological suffering using animals in laboratory settings found that helplessness can be taught easily and reversed with some effort. At the University of Pennsylvania, researchers found that if they shocked the floors of dogs' cages, after some effort at escape, the dogs simply curled up and took the abuse. Even after the dogs were shown how to escape the shock, many had learned that what they did made no difference in their plight and continued to be shocked. It took experimenters dozens of times of showing the dogs where safety could be found before the creatures would venture to the area that was not electrified. The problem was not the shock but, rather, the dogs' inability to do anything about it (Seligman, 1995).

 It appears to be quite easy to induce helplessness in humans.

These experiments have been performed on a number of creatures, including humans. In one such study, student volunteers were exposed to loud noises. One group could escape the noises; the other could not. When later given a learning task that would cause the noise to cease, the group who experienced the inescapable noises had more difficulty learning the task. It appears to be quite easy to induce helplessness in humans (Sapolsky, 2004).

To me, an even scarier study was one involving inner-city school students with severe reading problems. Psychologists taught these students a more complex language, Chinese. In a matter of hours the students were reading more complex symbolic sentences in Chinese than they could in English. Some of these students simply believed that they were incapable of learning (Sapolsky, 2004).

Here are some signs of learned helplessness:

- Lack of motivation
- Cognitive distortions—the glass is always half empty
- Apathy

- Increased sarcasm
- Unresponsive to new and interesting stimuli
- Feeling or perception of lack of control over situations
- Feeling of powerlessness

What is going on in the brain of the helpless student? Corticotropin releasing factor (CRF), the substance released by the hypothalamus to cause the release of stress hormones such as cortisol, is elevated. The release of cortisol may become continuous, eventually damaging the hippocampus. There are depletions of serotonin, dopamine, and norepinephrine. Norepinephrine is usually released when new stimuli are introduced into an individual's environment. In the helpless individual, there is a lack of interest and motivation. The immune system is depressed in these individuals, making them more vulnerable to illness (Giuffre & DiGeronimo, 1999).

Learned helplessness can be cured with effort, and fortunately, it can be prevented. To cure helplessness, students must be taught that their actions have effects. This may take great effort and repeated experiences to change the brain. Preventing helplessness must include early experiences with mastery (Seligman, 1995).

The key to this condition is control. When students feel that they have no control over their experiences, they may develop learned helplessness. Giving students more control in the classroom is a step toward prevention. In the case of students who believe they have no control, simply offering the option won't help. These students must experience being effective; this list provides some experiences you can give them in the classroom:

- Play games that require everyone's participation.
- Provide and discuss choices and consequences of those choices.
- Provide an agenda or preview of the day's activities to give students predictability and a feeling of control.
- Provide time for journaling and talking.
- Provide movement to release "feel-good" neurotransmitters.

Therapy may be necessary for some students with this disorder. Helpless students can become depressed. We must remember that it takes time to rewire the brain. Spending time with these students and addressing their negative thoughts and perceptions would be helpful. It is not always a perfect world in the classroom, and time is not always available; however, learned helplessness can be alleviated with time and effort. Be an optimistic role model for your students. They look up to you and may want to adopt your outlook.

The Attention Deficit Brain

Attention deficit disorder (ADD) is the most common neurobehavioral disorder of childhood and one of the most predominant chronic health conditions affecting school-age children. Yet some neuroscientists feel it is much underdiagnosed (Amen, 2005). Inattention, hyperactivity, and impulsivity are core symptoms. Academic underachievement, trouble with interpersonal relationships, and low self-esteem may be experienced as well. ADD is found in association with other disorders, such as oppositional-defiant disorder, conduct disorder, depression, and anxiety disorder, and also with speech and language delays and learning disabilities (American Academy of Pediatrics, 2000). Children with ADD continuously concentrate and focus on the newest or most demanding distraction that is present. About four million American children are taking medication, such as Ritalin, to treat this problem. Every day, stimulants are being prescribed for about 1,400 new children (DeGrandpre & Hinshaw, 2000).

> Attention deficit disorder (ADD) is the most common neurobehavioral disorder of childhood, and one of the most predominant chronic health conditions affecting school-age children. Yet some neuroscientists feel it is much underdiagnosed.

ADD is a condition that involves three problems in the behavioral and cognitive areas:

- The inability to focus attention for periods of time
- Difficulty in controlling impulses and delaying gratification
- Deficiency in controlling movement

Its diagnostic criteria include the following:

- Symptoms must begin before the age of seven.
- Symptoms must be persistent over time.
- Symptoms must be present in different situations.
- Problems must be extreme for the child's age and developmental level.

The causes of ADD include heredity. DR4R has been identified as a gene responsible for coding for the dopamine receptor. This is a susceptibility gene that may interact with the environment to create a potential for the disorder. Low birth weight for the child and smoking during pregnancy for the mother may be biological risk factors (DeGrandpre & Hinshaw, 2000).

What does an ADD brain look like? Imaging studies of these brains show a lack of activity in several areas of the right hemisphere. The anterior cingulate, which is associated with focusing attention, and the prefrontal cortex, which controls impulses and plans actions, are underactive. The integration of stimuli is thought to be controlled by an area in the upper auditory cortex that appears to be underactive as well (Carter, 1998).

Which of your students often exhibit the following behaviors?

- Leave work unfinished
- Have limited short-term memory
- Wiggle and jiggle
- Do not follow through on instructions
- Have difficulty waiting for their turns
- Interrupt
- Have difficulty engaging in quiet or leisurely activities
- Fail to think ahead and be prepared

The guidelines for the actual diagnosis of ADD have been clearly stated by the American Academy of Pediatrics (2000). They use explicit criteria, obtain information regarding the symptoms in more than one setting, and search for coexisting conditions. Treatment may include psychostimulants and behavior therapy.

Suggestions for dealing with students with this disorder include the following:

- Preview material up to a week in advance. Use attractive posters so students will view them when they are not attending to what the rest of the class is doing.
- Use the morning hours for short-term memory activities.
- Teach in a variety of ways, using the theory of multiple intelligences, to capitalize on student strengths.
- Set limits and rules and abide by them.
- Use positive reinforcement as much as possible.
- Create an inviting classroom and allow personal space to be individualized by each student.
- Role-model organizational skills.
- Provide movement opportunities.
- Introduce new material in a multisensory fashion (puppet shows, role-play, etc.).

Some have thought that students with ADD are overstimulated. Recent research suggests that they may be understimulated. They may require more stimulation than other children (Armstrong, 1999). Stimulation comes in many forms, including physical exercise. In a recent study, Caterino and Polak (1999) concluded that the level of focus and concentration in young children improves substantially after physical activity.

MAKING A DIFFERENCE

It is estimated that nearly 40 percent of our students suffer from some kind of learning impairment (Jensen, 2000b). In order to teach to such diverse groups, educators need background knowledge in how the brain works and how to cope with some of these disorders. Every brain has some of the same requirements. Sleep, proper nutrition, and exercise are among these. If our students arrive at school well nourished and well rested, we have a positive starting point.

> In order to teach to such diverse groups, educators need background knowledge in how the brain works and how to cope with some of these disorders.

Brain-research-based strategies have stood the test of time. Some of them enable us to teach a class of students, and many of them enable us to teach each student in a class. They enable us to see that although students' brains are unique, there are strategies available for teaching each.

It is Marnie's senior year in high school. School is still not always an easy place for her to be. A few weeks ago, Scott and I were out to dinner, and we ran into Marnie's second-grade teacher. I broke into a cold sweat!

Marnie has always wanted me to go to her schools and show her teachers the way I teach—but people don't seem to consider you an expert unless you live 25 miles away. I share with her the methods I know, hoping that she can help herself. We watch her struggle with classes and don't comment when our friends' kids bring home report cards. Marnie never seems to tell us when she gets her report card or any grades for that matter.

After a particularly trying day at school, I come home to an unusually happy child. Before I can get my coat off she says, "Mom, do you remember what you said you would give me for an A on my report card?" Before the days of research, I desperately tried to extrinsically motivate my daughter. "No, Marn, what did we offer you?" Her response is quick, "Twenty bucks!" Then it all comes back to me. We had told her that we would give her $20 for an A, $10 for a B, and then start deducting for lower grades. I could not remember ever having paid her.

I nod that I agree with her memory. She whips out her report card and starts laughing. Five subjects—five A's. It is remarkable. I look at my child in disbelief. "Did you know that you were doing this well?" She just smiles more broadly. "Do you know how you did this?"

As I take my charge card out of my wallet and hand it to her, she explains her accomplishment. "I knew I wouldn't have a problem in Mrs. K's class; she has us on teams. The other classes are traditional lecture, so I've been inviting my friends over to study. I borrow their notes and walk around the living room while we talk about the material. After I've walked and talked, I own that information." She takes my card, promises to spend only $100, and is on her way to the mall.

Marnie managed those A's one more time during that final year. She went on to a university and received a degree in history. When we offered to send her on for a master's degree she said, "This bachelor's degree is for you, Mom. I'm all schooled out. Now I'm going to find a place where I can be happy." She's done that. Her job involves lots of action and very little sitting still.

We're Off to See . . .

Your journey is almost over. From managing stress to eliciting positive states, you have taken a look at the whole child. Brain and body are never separate.

WIZDOM

Key Points to Ponder

1. Sleep is vital to learning and memory.

2. The brain cannot store energy; therefore breakfast is the most important meal of the day.

3. It is important to learn about the different brains in your classroom and be able to identify problems.

Suggestions

- Research suggests the importance of sleep for learning, so share a plan of action with your students. After learning, suggest that they review the material before bed, go to sleep, and review the material again after waking.
- Promoting movement in the classroom may not be real exercise, but keep in mind that it will get blood and oxygen to the brain to make students more alert.
- For information about ADD and other disorders, check the Web site of the American Academy of Pediatrics at http://www.aap.org.

10 Leaving the Land of Oz

With Courage, Passion, and Brains

How can you talk if you haven't got a brain?

—Dorothy

It is the end of the conference. I am in the lobby awaiting my turn at the checkout desk of the hotel. In front of me is the group I spoke to at lunch earlier in the conference about brain-compatible teaching and the Wizard of Oz analogy. One of the teachers turns around and smiles.

"How did you like the conference?" I ask politely. "I saw you in one of my sessions. I hope you got something out of it."

"Oh, I did!" she replies graciously. Of course, what else is she going to say? One thing I know about teachers—we're courteous!

Her friend turns at that comment. "I really liked it, too. I just hope I can remember some of it!"

I wince at that comment. National conferences are wonderful for getting overviews of information, but it really takes in-depth professional development to adopt a philosophy.

At that moment, Mr. Phillips, the principal walks over. "Can you recommend some follow-up reading on your topic? What's the name of that wizard book you wrote?" he asks. "We don't have much money, but I'd like to see if I can respark some interest in brain-compatible teaching."

I share the title with him and tell him the second edition will be out shortly. "My e-mail address is in the book," I mention. "If you get a book study going, I'd be happy to have some electronic conversations with your staff."

"Do you have time for that?" one teacher asks.

"I'll find time. I would have given up several times when I first started if I hadn't had some mentors. I hope you'll take me up on it."

We say our good-byes, and I wish them luck. As I taxi to the airport, I begin to look through my notes from the conference. My learning curve went up as I attended different sessions. I also pull out my reflections and evaluations from the preconference session I gave on *Becoming a "Wiz" at Brain-Based Teaching*—six hours with teachers who wanted to know more. In a full-day session, I feel that I can reach many of them on that emotional level where real learning takes place. I can give them enough "things to do on Monday" as well as share my philosophy and the principles of brain-based teaching. If I have the opportunity to meet with them again, I can reinforce those principles and help them apply the strategies in more depth.

I realize how lucky I am. I have had the opportunity to teach thousands of students, and I have learned from them as well. I am now training thousands of teachers who will teach thousands more students and change their lives. And every training is another learning experience for me.

The education-neuroscience connection is gaining strength. We have come far combining neuroscience, cognitive science, psychology, and education, and the results are clear: When we understand the way the brain learns, we can use teaching strategies that lead to success. Research indicates that the most influential component of raising student achievement is the teacher. Teaching at this time requires the courage, passion, and brains represented by the Lion, the Tin Man, and the Scarecrow. I wish you a safe and wonderful journey.

WIZDOM

I wrote about my daughter-in-law's pregnancy as I discussed the developing brain. I want you to know that Jackson Joseph Sprenger was born February eighth—a full-term healthy baby boy!

Glossary of Terms

Acetylcholine: A neurotransmitter involved in learning and memory. It is present at higher levels during sleep.

ACTH: Adrenocorticotropin hormone is released during stress by the pituitary gland.

Adagio: A slow tempo or movement, as in a symphony.

Amygdala: Almond-shaped structure in the limbic area of the brain that catalogs emotional memory.

Authentic assessment: An assessment associated with a real-life task.

Automatic memory: This memory pathway is a conditioned response or reflexive memory.

Axon: The long nerve fiber on a neuron that sends messages to other neurons.

Brain stem: Also called the reptilian brain. This is the lower level of the brain where information enters.

Cerebellum: Also called the little brain. Located at the base of the brain, this structure is linked to posture, balance, coordination, and some memory.

Cerebrum: This structure consists of the right and left hemispheres. It has four lobes: frontal, parietal, occipital, and temporal.

Cingulate gyrus: This structure mediates information between the cortex and the limbic structures. It is located between them.

Conditioned response memory: *See* Automatic memory.

Corpus callosum: A bundle of nerve fibers connecting the left and right hemispheres.

Cortisol: The stress hormone secreted by the adrenal glands during stress.

CRF: Corticotropin releasing factor. This chemical is secreted by the hypothalamus. It causes the pituitary gland to release ACTH.

Dendrite: Thin fiber that grows from the cell body of the neuron. It receives information from other neurons.

Dopamine: A neurotransmitter involved in mood and movement.

Electroencephalogram: Usually referred to as an EEG. It records your brain wave activity when you are concentrating, asleep, and awake.

Emotional memory: Memory dealing with feelings. It is cataloged through the amygdala.

Endorphin: A neurotransmitter, endogenous morphine, the body's natural painkiller.

Enkephalin: Involved in pain and pleasure, this peptide neurotransmitter is part of the endogenous morphine system.

Enteric nervous system: The local nervous system of the digestive tract.

Episodic memory: Memory involving location that is stored through the hippocampus.

Eustress: Mild, positive stress.

fMRI: A procedure that uses magnetic resonance imaging to generate images that reflect which structures in the brain are activated (and how) during performance of different tasks.

GABA: Gamma-aminobutyric acid, a neurotransmitter that prevents neurons from firing.

Glial cell: Brain cell that supports neurons.

Glutamate: Plentiful neurotransmitter involved with activating neurons.

Hippocampus: Seahorse-shaped structure involved with factual memory.

Homeostasis: The literal meaning is "keeping things the same." In maintaining this state, the body and brain seek to keep balance.

HPA axis: The hypothalamus-pituitary-adrenal axis is the system that responds to stress. Its final products, corticosteroids, target components of the limbic system, particularly the hippocampus.

Hypothalamus: Located beneath the thalamus, this structure regulates internal information.

Interneuron: A nerve cell found entirely within the nervous system that acts as a link between sensory and motor neurons.

Limbic brain: A group of structures in the brain associated with memory and emotions.

Mammillary bodies: Memory processing structures connected to the hippocampus.

MRI: Magnetic resonance imaging, a technique that uses a magnetic field to map brain structure.

Myelin: White fatty substance that coats the axons of most neurons. It speeds transmission of messages.

Neocortex: The top layer of the cerebrum, in which higher-level thinking occurs.

Neural network: A connection among neurons that forms a pattern.

Neuron: The nerve cell of the brain involved in learning.

Neurotransmitters: Chemicals produced in neurons to send messages.

Norepinephrine: A neurotransmitter involved in our state of arousal.

Parasympathetic nervous system: This system is concerned with conservation and restoration of energy. It causes a reduction in heart rate and blood pressure and facilitates digestion, absorption of nutrients, and excretion of waste products.

Performance assessment: The demonstration of a skill or behavior using a rubric.

PET scan: Positron emission tomography, a brain-imaging technique that uses radioactive glucose to measure the amount of glucose used by various areas of the brain during specific tasks.

Pineal gland: This gland regulates the release of neurotransmitters in charge of sleep.

Pituitary gland: The gland that runs the endocrine system. It is involved in the stress response.

Plasticity: The brain's ability to change.

Portfolio: A collection of student work showing progress over time. It may be used for assessment or reflection.

Procedural memory: Muscle memory, the long-term memory of skills and procedures.

Reptilian brain: Another term for brain stem, the most primitive area of the brain.

Rubric: An assessment instrument using specific criteria to create and assess a performance or product.

Semantic memory: Factual memory associated with the hippocampus.

Serotonin: A neurotransmitter involved in regulating mood.

SPECT scan: Single photon emission computed tomography, a nuclear imaging test that shows blood flow.

Sympathetic nervous system: This system enables the body to be prepared for fear, fight, or flight.

Synapse: The space between the axon of the sending neuron and the dendrite of the receiving neuron.

Thalamus: This structure in the limbic area of the brain sorts messages.

Triune brain theory: The three-system theory of the brain developed by Dr. Paul MacLean.

References and Supplementary Reading

Ackerman, D. (2004). *An alchemy of mind.* New York: Scribner.

Adler, J. (1998). Tomorrow's child. *Newsweek, 132*(18), 54.

Amen, D. (1998). *Change your brain, change your life.* New York: Times Books/Random House.

Amen, D. (2005). *Making a good brain great.* New York: Random House.

American Academy of Pediatrics. (2000). Clinical practice guideline: Diagnosis and evaluation of the child with attention-deficit/hyperactivity disorder. *Pediatrics, 105,* 1158–1170.

American Dietetic Association. (2006). *Dietary guidance for healthy children aged 2 to 11 years.* Retrieved March, 2006, from http://www.eatright.org/cps/rde/xchg/ada/hs.xsl/advocacy_3778_ENU_HTML.htm

Anderson, L., Krathwohl, D., Airasian, P., Cruikshank, K., Mayer, R., Pintrich, P., et al. (Eds.). (2001). *A taxonomy for learning, teaching, and assessing.* New York: Longman.

Armstrong, T. (1998). *Awakening genius in the classroom.* Alexandria, VA: Association for Supervision and Curriculum Development.

Armstrong, T. (1999). *ADD/ADHD alternatives in the classroom.* Alexandria, VA: Association for Supervision and Curriculum Development.

Barber, J., Barrett, K., Beals, K., Bergman, L., & Diamond, M. (1999). *Learning about learning.* Berkeley, CA: Lawrence Hall of Science.

Barnet, A., & Barnet, R. (1998). *The youngest minds.* New York: Simon & Schuster.

Benard, B. (2004). *Resiliency: What we have learned.* San Francisco: WestEd.

Benesh, B. (Developer). (1999). *The human brain inquiry kit.* Alexandria, VA: Association for Supervision and Curriculum Development.

Bergmann, S. (2005). *Experts urge students to make time for breakfast.* Retrieved March, 2006, from http://www.mercedsearch.com/news/239.html

Blum, D. (1998, October). Face it. *Psychology Today, 31,* 32–39, 66–70.

Blum, D. (1999). More work, more play. *Mother Jones* [Electronic version]. Retrieved December 6, 2004, from http://www.motherjones.com/news/feature/1999/03/blum.html

Bower, B. (2000). Grade-schoolers grow into sleep loss. *Science News, 157*(21), 324.

Brink, S. (2000). Sleepless society. *U.S. News & World Report, 129*(15), 62–72.

Brooks, M. (1989). *Instant rapport.* New York: Warner Books.

Brooks, M. (1999). Creating a positive school climate. In J. Cohen (Ed.), *Educating minds and hearts*. Alexandria, VA: Association for Supervision and Curriculum Development.

Brothers, L. (1997). *Friday's footprint*. New York: Oxford University Press.

Brownlee, S. (1996). The biology of soul murder. *U.S. News & World Report, 121*, 71–73.

Brownlee, S. (1999). Inside the teen brain. *U.S. News & World Report, 127*(6), 44–54.

Burke, K. (2000). *How to assess authentic learning*, 3rd ed. Upper Saddle River, NJ: Prentice Hall.

Buzan, T. (2000). *Head first*. Glasgow, Scotland: Bath Press Colourbooks.

Calvin, W. (1996). *How brains think*. New York: Basic Books/HarperCollins.

Carnegie, D. (1936). *How to win friends and influence people*. New York: Pocket Books.

Carper, J. (2000). *Your miracle brain*. New York: HarperCollins.

Carskadon, M. A. (1995). *A prominent sleep researcher says staying awake may be overrated*. Retrieved August, 2004, from http://www.brown.edu/Administration/Brown_Alumni_Magaxine/96/12–95/elms/qa.html

Carter, R. (1998). *Mapping the mind*. Los Angeles: University of California Press.

Casanova, U., & Berliner, D. (1986). Should students be made test-wise? *Instructor, 95*(6), 22–23.

Caterino, M. C., & Polak, E. (1999). Effects of two types of activity on the performance of second-, third-, and fourth-grade students on a test of concentration. *Perceptual & Motor Skills, 89*, 245–248.

Chudler, E. (1998). Salty what? Saltatory conduction. *Neuroscience for Kids*. Retrieved May, 1998, from http://faculty.washington.edu/chudler/neurok.html

Chudler, E. (1999). Glia: The forgotten brain cell. *Neuroscience for Kids*. Retrieved February, 2000, from http://facultywashington.edu/chudier/neurok.html

Cohen, J. (1999). *Educating minds and hearts*. Alexandria, VA: Association for Supervision and Curriculum Development.

Covey, S. (1990). *The 7 habits of highly effective people*. New York: Fireside.

Cromie, W. (2001). Music on the brain: Researchers explore the biology of music. *Harvard University Gazette* (March 21, 2001). Retrieved April, 2002, from http://www.news.harvard.edu/gazette/2001/03.22/04-music.html

Damasio, A. (1999). *The feeling of what happens*. New York: Harcourt Brace.

Dana Alliance for Brain Initiatives. (1998). *Gray matters: The teenage brain* [Radio broadcast]. Minneapolis, MN: Public Radio International. Retrieved August, 2006, from http://www. dana.org/pdf/other/graymat_teenage.pdf

DeFina, P. (2003, November). *The neurobiology of memory: Understand, apply, and assess student memory*. Presentation at the Learning and the Brain Conference, Cambridge, MA.

DeGrandpre, R., & Hinshaw, S. (2000). ADHD: Serious psychiatric problem or all-American copout? *Cerebrum, 2*(3), 12–36.

Dement, W., & Vaughan, C. (1999). *The promise of sleep*. New York: Delacorte.

Dennison, P., & Dennison, G. (1994). *Brain gym* (Teacher's ed., Rev.). Ventura, CA: Edu-Kinesthetics.

Diamond, M. (1999a). *Brains and education: A partnership for life* [Audiotape]. Alexandria, VA: Association for Supervision and Curriculum Development.

Diamond, M. (1999b). *How new knowledge about the brain improves school learning* [Audiotape]. Alexandria, VA: Association for Supervision and Curriculum Development.

Diamond, M., & Hopson, J. (1998). *Magic trees of the mind.* New York: Dutton.

Elias, M., & Arnold, H. (Eds.). (2006). *The educator's guide to emotional intelligence and academic achievement.* Thousand Oaks, CA: Corwin Press.

Eliot, L. (1999). *What's going on in there?* New York: Bantam.

Faber, A., & Mazlish, E. (1995). *How to talk so kids can learn.* New York: Rawson.

Fallone, G., Acebo, C., Seifer, R., & Carskadon, M. A. (2005). Experimental restriction of sleep opportunity in children: Effects on teacher ratings. *Sleep, 28*(12), 1561–1567.

Fauber, J. (1999). Abuse can rewire kids' brains. *The Brain in the News, 6*(10), 1.

Feinstein, S. (2004). *Secrets of the teen brain.* Thousand Oaks, CA: Corwin Press.

Fischer, J. S. (1999). From Romania, a lesson in resilience. *U.S. News & World Report, 127*(10), 50.

Fogarty, R. (2001). *Brain-compatible classrooms* (3rd ed.). Thousand Oaks, CA: Corwin Press.

Gardner, H. (1985). *Frames of mind: The theory of multiple intelligences.* New York: Basic Books.

Gardner, H. (2000). *Intelligence reframed: Multiple intelligences for the 21st century.* New York: Basic Books.

Giedd, J. (2002). *Frontline: Inside the teenage brain* [Video recording]. Boston, MA: PBS.

Giuffre, K., & DiGeronimo, T. (1999). *The care and feeding of your brain.* Franklin Lakes, NJ: Career Press.

Gladwell, M. (2002). *The tipping point.* New York: Little, Brown.

Glasser, W. (1992). *The quality school.* New York: HarperCollins.

Glenn, S. H. (1989). *Raising self-reliant children in a self-indulgent world.* Rocklin, CA: Prima.

Glenn, H. S. (1990). *The greatest human need* [Video recording]. Gold River, CA: Capabilities.

Goleman, D. (1995). *Emotional intelligence.* New York: Bantam.

Goleman, D. (1998a). *Emotional intelligence: A new model for curriculum development* [Audiotape]. Alexandria, VA: Association for Supervision and Curriculum Development.

Goleman, D. (1998b). *Working with emotional intelligence.* New York: Bantam.

Goleman, D., Boyatzis, R., & Mckee., A. (2002). *Primal leadership.* Boston: Harvard Business School Press.

Gopnik, A., Meltzoff, A., & Kuhl, P. (1999). *The scientist in the crib.* New York: William Morrow.

Graham, R. (1999). Unnannounced quizzes raise test scores selectively for mid-range students. *Teaching of Psychology, 26*(4), 271–273.

Grinder, M. (1991). *Righting the educational conveyor belt.* Portland, OR: Metamorphous.

Guild, P., & Garger, S. (1998). *Marching to different drummers* (2nd ed.). Alexandria, VA: Association for Supervision and Curriculum Development.

Gurian, M., & Ballew, A. (2003). *The boys and girls learn differently action guide for teachers.* San Francisco: Jossey-Bass.

Hamer, D., & Copeland, P. (1998). *Living with our genes.* New York: Doubleday.

Hannaford, C. (2005). *Smart moves.* Arlington, VA: Great River Books.

Hayden, T. (2000, Fall & Winter). A sense of self. *Newsweek* (Special ed.), pp. 56–62.

Healy, J. (2004). *Your child's growing mind* (3rd ed.). New York: Broadway Books.

Holloway, J. (2000). How does the brain learn science? *Educational Leadership, 58*(3), 85–86.

Hooper, J., & Teresi, D. (1986). *The 3-pound universe.* New York: Putnam.

Howard, P. (1994). *The owner's manual for the brain.* Austin, TX: Leornian.

Howard, P. (1999). *The owner's manual for the brain* (2nd ed.). Austin, TX: Bard.

Howard, P. (2006). *The owner's manual for the brain* (3rd ed.). Austin, TX: Bard.

Human Genome Project. (1990–2003). Retrieved December, 2005, from http://www .ornl.gov/sci/techresources/Human_Genome/home.shtml

Hyman, S. (1999). *Susceptibility and second hits.* In R. Conlan (Ed.), *States of mind* (pp. 9–28). New York: Wiley.

Jacobs, H. (2004). *Getting results with curriculum mapping.* Alexandria, VA: Association for Supervision and Curriculum Development.

Jensen, E. (1998). *Teaching with the brain in mind.* Alexandria, VA: Association for Supervision and Curriculum Development.

Jensen, E. (1999). *Insights for better classroom management from brain research* [Audiotape]. Alexandria, VA: Association for Supervision and Curriculum Development.

Jensen, E. (2000a). *Brain-based learning.* Thousand Oaks, CA: Corwin Press.

Jensen, E. (2000b). *Different brains, different learners.* Thousand Oaks, CA: Corwin Press.

Jensen, E. (2000c). *Learning with the body in mind.* Thousand Oaks, CA: Corwin Press.

Jensen, E. (2000d). *Music with the brain in mind.* Thousand Oaks, CA: Corwin Press.

Jensen, E. (2005). *Teaching with the brain in mind* (2nd ed.). Alexandria, VA: Association for Supervision and Curriculum Development.

Johnson, S. (2004). *Mind wide open: Your brain and the science of everyday life.* New York: Scribner.

Jourdain, R. (1997). *Music, the brain, and ecstasy.* New York: Avon.

Kandel, E. (September, 2004). *Genes and the brain.* Cambridge, MA: Lichtenstein Creative Media. Retrieved January, 2005, from http://www.lcmedia.com/mind340.htm

Kantrowitz, B., & Underwood, A. (1999). Dyslexia and the new science of reading. *Newsweek, 133*(21), 72–78.

Kelly, K. (2000). Today's kids: overscheduled and overtired. *U.S. News & World Report, 129*(15), 66.

Kids and breakfast. (2003). Retrieved February, 2006, from http://www.keepkidshealthy .com/nutrition/breakfast.html

Klein, J. D. (1997). The national longitudinal study on adolescent health. *Journal of the American Medical Association, 278*(10), 854–859.

Klingberg, T., Forssberg, H., & Westerberg, H. (2002). Training of working memory in children with ADHD. *Journal of Clinical & Experimental Neuropsychology, 24,* 781–791.

Kobasa, S. O. (1979). Stressful life events, personality, and health: An inquiry into hardiness. *Journal of Personality and Social Psychology, 37,* 1–11.

Kohn, A. (1993). *Punished by rewards.* New York: Houghton Mifflin.

Kotulak, R. (1996). *Inside the brain.* Kansas City, MO: Andrews and McMeel.

Kotulak, R. (2004, May 2). Scientists offer hope for poor readers. *The Chicago Tribune,* p. C1.

Kubow, R., Wahlstrom, K., & Bemis, A. (1999). Starting time and school life: Reflections from educators and students. In K. Wahlstrom (Ed.), *Adolescent sleep needs and school starting times* (pp. 61–77). Bloomington, IN: Phi Delta Kappa.

Kunzig, R. (1998). Climbing through the brain. *Discover, 19*(8), 61–69.

LeDoux, J. (2002). *The synaptic self.* New York: Simon & Schuster.

Mahoney, D., & Restak, R. (1998). *The longevity strategy.* New York: Dana.

Mann, L. (1999). Dance education: The ultimate sport. *Education Update, 41*(5), 41.

Margulies, N., & Sylwester, R. (1998). *Emotion and learning.* Tucson, AZ: Zephyr.

Marzano, R. (2000). *Transforming classroom grading.* Alexandria, VA: Association for Supervision and Curriculum Development.

Marzano, R. (2004). *Building background knowledge for academic achievement: Research on what works in schools.* Alexandria, VA: Association for Supervision and Curriculum Development.

Marzano, R., Pickering, D., & Pollack, J. (2001). *Classroom instruction that works.* Alexandria, VA: Association for Supervision and Curriculum Development.

McCormick Tribune Foundation. (2004). *What every child needs* [DVD]. Chicago: Chicago Production Center.

McEwen, B. (1999). Stress and the brain. In R. Conlan (Ed.), *States of mind* (pp. 81–101). New York: Wiley.

McEwen, B. & Lasley, E. (2001). *The end of stress as we know it.* Washington, DC: The Dana Press.

McPherson, F. (2004). *The memory key.* New York: Barnes & Noble.

National Institute of Mental Health. (2000). *Depression in children and adolescents* [Electronic edition]. Publication No. 004744. Bethesda, MD: Author. Retrieved December, 2000, from http://www.nimh.nih.gov

National Reading Panel. (2000). *An evidence-based assessment of the scientific research literature on reading and its implications for reading instruction.* Washington, DC: National Institute of Child Health and Human Development.

Neville, H. (1997). Old brain/new tricks. In *Ask the scientists* [Web site]. Retrieved December, 1999, from http://www.pbs.org/safarchive/3_ask/archive/qna/3273_hneville.html

Niehoff, D. (1999). *The biology of violence.* New York: Free Press.

Oliveira, R. (1999, June 6). No time to share. *Standard Times.* Retrieved August, 2006, from http://www.s-t.com/daily/06–99/06–06–99/a01lo004.htm

Payne, R. (2005). *A framework for understanding poverty.* Highlands, TX: aha! Process Inc.

Perkins, D. (1995). *Outsmarting IQ.* New York: Free Press.

Pert, C. (1997). *Molecules of emotion.* New York: Scribner.

Peterson, C., & Seligman, M. (2003). *Values in action classification of strengths.* Washington, DC: American Psychological Association and Oxford, UK: Oxford University Press.

Pratt, S., & Matthews, K. (2004). *Super foods r/x.* New York: HarperCollins.

Quenk, R. (1997). *The spirit that moves us.* Gardiner, ME: Tilbury House.

Ramey, C., & Ramey, S. (1999). *Right from birth.* New York: Goddard.

Ratey, J. (2000). *Care and feeding of the brain* [Audiotape]. Boston: Public Information Resources.

Ratey, J. (2001). *A user's guide to the brain.* New York: Pantheon.

Restak, R. (2000). *Mysteries of the mind.* Washington, DC: National Geographic Society.

Roizen, M., & Oz, M. (2005). *You: The owner's manual.* New York: HarperCollins.

Rose, C., & Nicholl, M. (1997). *Accelerated learning for the 21st century.* New York: Dell.

Rupp, R. (1998). *Committed to memory: How we remember and why we forget.* New York: Crown.

Sapolsky, R. (1999). *How new knowledge about the brain improves school learning.* [Audiotape]. Alexandria, VA: Association for Supervision and Curriculum Development.

Sapolsky, R. (2004). *Why zebras don't get ulcers.* New York: Freeman.

Sapolsky, R. (2005). Sick of poverty. *Scientific American, 293,* 92–99.

Seligman, M. (1990). *Learned optimism.* New York: Pocket Books.

Seligman, M. (1995). *The optimistic child.* Boston: Houghton Mifflin.

Seuss, Dr., Johnson, S., & Fancher, L. (1998). *My many colored days.* New York: Knopf.

Shaywitz, S. (2003). *Overcoming dyslexia.* New York: Knopf.

Shimamura, A. P. (2000). The role of the prefrontal cortex in dynamic filtering [Electronic version]. *Psychobiology, 28,* 207–218. Retrieved December, 2005, from http://ist-socrates.berkeley.edu/shimlab/ShimPubs.html

Snowdon, D. (2001). *Aging with grace.* New York: Bantam.

Sousa, D. (2006). *How the brain learns* (3rd ed.). Thousand Oaks, CA: Corwin Press.

Sprenger, M. (1999). *Learning and memory. The brain in action.* Alexandria, VA: Association for Supervision and Curriculum Development.

Sprenger, M. (2003). *Differentiation through learning styles and memory.* Thousand Oaks, CA: Corwin Press.

Sprenger, M. (2005). *How to teach so students remember.* Alexandria, VA: Association for Supervision and Curriculum Development.

Stern, P., & Carstensen, L. (Eds.). (2000). *The aging mind: Opportunities in cognitive research.* Washington, DC: National Academy Press.

Sternberg, E. (2000). *The balance within: The science connecting health and emotions.* New York: Freeman.

Stiggins, R., Arter, J., Chappuis, J., & Chappuis, S. (2005). *Classroom assessment for student learning: Doing it right, using it well.* Portland, OR: ATI.

Sturrock, C. (2005, November 17). Playing music can be good for your brain. *San Francisco Chronicle* [Electronic version]. Retrieved May, 2006, from http://www.sfgate.com/cgi-bin/article.cgi?f=/c/a/2005/11/17/MNGQ9FPODP1.DTL

Sylwester, R. (1995). *A celebration of neurons.* Alexandria, VA: Association for Supervision and Curriculum Development.

Sylwester, R. (1997a). *Applying brain stress research to classroom management* [Audiotape]. Alexandria, VA: Association for Supervision and Curriculum Development.

Sylwester, R. (1997b). The neurobiology of self-esteem and aggression. *Educational Leadership, 54*(5), 75–79.

Sylwester, R. (2000). *A biological brain in a cultural classroom.* Thousand Oaks, CA: Corwin Press.

Talaga, T. (2000). Rethinking the brain. *The Brain in the News, 7*(6), 3.

Tallal, P. (1999). *How new knowledge about the brain improves school learning.* [Audiotape]. Alexandria, VA: Association for Supervision and Curriculum Development.

Taylor, S. E., Klein, L. C., Lewis, B. P., Gruenewald, T. L., Gurung, R. A. R., & Updegraff, J. A. (2000). Biobehavioral responses to stress in females: Tend-and-befriend, not fight-or-flight. *Psychological Review, 107,* 441–429.

Tyre, P. (2005). Boy brains, girl brains. *Newsweek, 146*(12), 59.

University of Minnesota, College of Education and Human Development. (1997). *School start-time study.* Retrieved August, 2006, from http://www.education.umn.edu/CAREI/Reports/summary.html

U.S. Department of Health and Human Services. (1993). *Eighth special report to the U.S. Congress on alcohol and health.* Washington, DC: Author.

Walsh, D. (2004). *Why do they act that way?* New York: Free Press.

Weinberger, D., Elvevag, B., & Giedd, J. (2005). *The adolescent brain: A work in progress.* Washington, DC: National Campaign to Prevent Teen Pregnancy.

Werner, E., & Smith, R. (1992). *Overcoming the odds.* Ithaca, NY: Cornell University Press.

Werner, E., & Smith, R. (2001). *Journeys from childhood to the midlife: Risk, resilience, and recovery.* Ithaca, NY: Cornell University Press.

Whitaker, J. (1999). *The memory solution.* New York: Avery.

Wiggins, G., & McTighe, J. (2005). *Understanding by design* (2nd ed.). Alexandria, VA: Association for Supervision and Curriculum Development.

Wilkinson, R. (2000). *Mind the gap: Hierarchies, health and human evolution.* London: Weidenfeld and Nicolson.

Wilson, M. A., & McNaughton, B. L. (1994). Reactivation of hippocampal ensemble memories during sleep. *Science, 265,* 676–679.

Wood, C. (2005). *Yardsticks: Responsive classrooms.* Turners Falls, MA: Northeast Foundation for Children.

Zins, J., Weissberg, R., Wang, M., & Walberg, H. (Eds.). (2004). *Building academic success on social and emotional learning: What does the research say?* New York: Teachers College Press.

Index